Doing
Business
with
Japan

D0963550

Doing
Business
with
Japan

Successful Strategies for Intercultural Communication

Kazuo Nishiyama

A Latitude 20 Book
University of Hawai'i Press
Honolulu

Library of Congress Cataloging-in-Publication Data
Nishiyama, Kazuo.
Doing business with Japan: successful strategies for
intercultural communication/Kazuo Nishiyama.
p.   cm.
"Latitude 20 book."
Includes bibliographical references (p.).
ISBN 0–8248–2127–0 (pbk.:alk.paper)
1. Business etiquette—Japan.   2. Negotiation in business—Japan.
3. Corporate culture—Japan.   4. National characteristics, Japanese.
5. Intercultural communication—Japan.   6. United States—Commerce—Japan.
7. Japan—Commerce—United States.   I. Title.
HF5389.3.J3N57 2000
395.5'2'0952—dc21   99–30350
                                                                CIP

University of Hawai'i Press books are printed on acid-free paper and meet the
guidelines for permanence and durability of the Council on Library Resources.

Printed by The Maple-Vail Book Manufacturing Group
Designed by Nina Lisowski

Contents

Acknowledgments

During my research and writing, many academic colleagues generously provided me with valuable advice and assistance. I am particularly grateful to Dr. James Mak and Dr. Larry Cross for their constructive suggestions for improving the first draft of this book.

I owe a special debt of gratitude to Ms. Judith Mills, who patiently and carefully edited subsequent drafts. She also has given me the advantage of her American perspective, offering very practical advice on how to adapt my writing to answer the many questions that Westerners may have about Japan and Japanese businesspeople.

Finally, I wish to thank my editor at the University of Hawai'i Press, Ms. Sharon Yamamoto, and Ms. Ann Ludeman, managing editor, for their expert assistance.

Introduction

Japan is the second-largest economic superpower, second only to the United States. Consumers in almost every country seek out products manufactured in Japan, such as automobiles, electronic home appliances, television sets, stereo players, transistor radios, digital cameras, and compact disc players. Japanese tourist spending has become a very important factor in world economics and an extremely important "intangible export" for many tourism-oriented countries.

In Japan, skyscraper office towers, Western-style hotels and restaurants, freeways full of cars, high-speed trains, slick subways, supermodern international airports, highly automated and productive factories, American fast-food chains, and Western entertainment and sports provide the impression that Japan is truly Westernized. However, Japan has selectively adopted only those aspects of Western culture that are useful and convenient. Despite appearances, Japan has remained "uniquely Japanese." For this reason, many uninformed Western businesspeople doing business in Japan will find it difficult and even frustrating to work with their Japanese counterparts unless they gain a good understanding of Japan and its people.

A brief look at its history will help explain why Japan has been interacting with other countries as it has in business and politics. The Tokugawa shogunate, founded by Tokugawa Ieyasu in 1600, viewed Christianity as subversive and foreign trade as dangerous to the stability of its feudal government. Tokugawa Ieyasu imposed the seclusion of Japan from all foreign contact for more than two centuries between 1638 and 1853. His successor, Tokugawa Hidetada, banned all missionary activity and expelled all European missionaries. The persecution of Christianity came to a climax between 1637 and 1638 when some twenty thousand Christian peasants who rose up in revolt were slaughtered at the old castle on Shimabara Peninsula. The Shimabara revolt marked the virtual end of Christianity in Japan. Starting in 1640, all Japanese were forced to register at local Buddhist temples so that the local governments could check on their religious affiliations. The Tokugawa government also closely controlled foreign trade to prevent local vassals from obtaining guns and other weapons from the West that might be used for subversive military activities. In 1633, all Japanese were prohibited on threat of death from going abroad or, if they were already abroad, from returning home.

2

The long period of continued isolation imposed by the Tokugawa government gave the Japanese a strong sense of self-identity. They came to view the rest of the world, including their close cultural and racial relatives in Korea and China, as "other," setting up an "us" versus "them" dichotomy. They still have a mania about distinguishing between "foreign" borrowing and elements regarded as "native" Japanese. Isolation produced a high degree of cultural and racial homogeneity in Japan. This prolonged separation from the outside world was indeed instrumental in spreading uniform cultural patterns throughout the Japanese islands and preventing the mixing of races for many generations. By turning inward on their own resources, the Japanese were able to develop fully their own cultural identity, distinctive personality traits, social skills, and artistic achievements.

On the other hand, the long isolation severely curtailed Japan's modernization and industrialization. The Japanese were humiliated by the industrialized Western powers. By the middle of the nineteenth century, steam-powered ships from Western nations came to display their advanced economic and military powers around the shores of Japan. In July 1853, a fleet of huge iron ships under the command of Commodore Matthew C. Perry steamed into Uraga near the mouth of Tokyo Bay. The Japanese called these iron ships *kurobune* or "black ships," and they were very frightened at the sight of them bellowing black smoke. In February 1854, Perry returned to Japan with a larger and more formidable squadron to demonstrate the might and determination of the

United States to pry open Japanese seaports for foreign ships. After a month of negotiations, the first treaty was signed, but it achieved only limited success. By this time, the Tokugawa government learned how badly the Chinese had been defeated by the mighty British navy warships in the Opium War of 1841 and realized that their small wooden vessels and antiquated shore batteries were no match for the American steam frigates equipped with huge modern cannons. The Japanese leaders knew that they would have to give in to foreign demands if they wanted to avoid the same fate that the Chinese had suffered. Townsend Harris, the American consul who was permitted to reside in Japan under this agreement, finally managed to negotiate a full trade treaty in 1858.

This event brought about the collapse of the Tokugawa shogunate and provided an impetus for the start of the Meiji Restoration of 1868. This was the restoration of the power of the emperor carried out in the name of Emperor Meiji and the establishment of a new form of government patterned after Western models. Several Japanese political leaders realized that the only defense against the West was to adopt its superior industrial and military technology. Under the slogan Rich Country, Strong Military *(fukoku kyōhei)*, they were bent on building a rich industrialized nation and a strong military, like the rich Western nations that were colonizing neighboring Asian countries. They worked feverishly to adopt Western military techniques. In fact, Japan began borrowing almost everything from the advanced Western countries. The Japanese government brought many experts from the United States and Europe to Japan at an exorbitant cost and had them teach eager Japanese students whatever expertise and knowledge they had: industrial technology, weaponry, navigation, commerce and trade, railways, telegraph, political and judicial systems, education, medicine, cuisine, fashion, art and literature, religion, and even farming.

Social changes also occurred under another slogan, Civilization and Enlightenment *(bunmeikaika)*. The Japanese began to imitate Western customs and social behavior. However, to retain national pride and to abate a sense of inferiority in the midst of massive foreign borrowing, the Japanese coined another slogan, Japanese Spirit, Western Technology *(wakon yōsai)*. It reminded the Japanese that retaining a Japanese spirit at heart was necessary for any successful adoption of Western technology. Even today, this slogan continues to be used by Japanese multinational corporations as a vehicle for corporate pride and national identity. In the corporate context, the slogan means that the Japanese must work diligently based on the Japanese work ethics of dedication and self-sacrifice, even though they may be using technological knowledge of Western origin. This was also a pragmatic and utilitarian approach to adopting Western technology without making drastic changes in traditional Japanese values.

Japan is a chain of narrow islands off the east coast of the huge continental land mass of China, the Korean Peninsula, and the former Soviet Union. The islands are surrounded by the vast sweep of the Pacific Ocean on the east, the Sea of Okhotsk on the north, the Sea of Japan on the west, and the Philippine Sea on the south. The country has the general shape of a crescent and extends 1,860 miles from the northern tip to the southern tip of the island chains. The total land area is 146,000 square miles and is made up of four major islands—Honshū, Hokkaido, Kyushu and Shikoku—and includes more than 4,000 smaller islands. These islands are collectively referred to as the Japanese Archipelago. The entire land area, however, is only one-twenty-fifth that of the United States or approximately the size of the State of Montana. Japan has a great variety of topographical features because it has several high volcanic mountain ranges running through the country. About 67 percent of Japan's land area is mountainous; agricultural land accounts for less than 20 percent, and only 3 percent is suitable for residential use. Another 10 percent is devoted to industrial production and infrastructure.

Japan's population is estimated to be 125,600,000, and the population density is more than 850 persons per square mile. Approximately 70 percent of the population lives on the strip of plains on the Pacific coast between the northern part of Kyushu and Honshū, where the weather is mild and where major cities and industrial facilities are most highly developed. In fact, three large metropolitan regions centered on Tokyo-Yokohama, Nagoya, and Osaka-Kobe-Kyoto hold 45 percent of the Japanese population. For example, Tokyo has 12 million people living in an area of 836 square miles, and Yokohama has 8 million people in an area of 928 square miles. Osaka has 8.7 million people in an area of 722 square miles. The unique feature of Japan's population is homogeneity; 99.4 percent of the population are ethnic Japanese, 0.5 percent Koreans, and 0.1 percent Chinese. The Koreans and Chinese are the descendants of migrant laborers who were brought to Japan at the beginning of the twentieth century and during World War II. They are alien residents of Japan, but a large majority of them have been culturally assimilated into Japanese society and have lost the ability to speak their native language.

Japan is a democratic country, but Japanese democracy is not the same as that of the United States. It is influenced by Japan's traditional culture and social customs. For example, decision making is not based on open public debate and discussion, but on consesus and intense behind-the-scene negotiations. The Japanese Diet is divided into two houses, the lower house or House of Representatives and the upper house or House of Councilors. The lower house drafts all laws and amendments, establishes budgets, and ratifies treaties. It also selects the prime minister who, in turn, selects the cabinet ministers. The upper house does not have any real power; it functions only as a check on actions of the lower house. The prime minister is chosen from among the strong leaders of the ruling party through intense negotiations among several factions within the party. Japanese politics has traditionally been controlled by career bureaucrats, not by politicians. Many influential Japanese political leaders are former high government officials. In fact, several of the most powerful prime ministers in recent years were former vice ministers who had served under politician-ministers. Former bureaucrats-turned-politicians have extensive interpersonal networks in both executive and administrative branches of the government, and they try to perpetuate the bureaucratic dominance. In essence, Japanese politics is *kanryō seiji* or "politics by bureaucrats."

5

Japan has the highest literacy rate in the world because of its excellent educational system. Attainment of this high literacy was facilitated by Japan's homogeneity in language, culture, and ethnicity and by its compact land area. Having only one language is a tremendous advantage for Japan, since there is no need to use other languages in instruction and publication. The central Ministry of Education approves all textbooks, specifies exactly what subjects are to be taught, and distributes a very detailed curriculum for each course for all elementary and junior high schools. All teachers are licensed by the Ministry of Education and are required to teach using the guidelines provided by the ministry. Uniformity, not diversity, is encouraged throughout the Japanese educational system, although a certain amount of diversity is allowed at university-level education.

All Japanese educational institutions are hierarchically ranked in quality of education and prestige. Because a student's success in life is practically determined by which university he graduates from, he devotes himself to studying from a very early age so that he can get into the best and most prestigious university. His family will make financial sacrifices to provide him with a tutor or send him to a *juken juku* (also called *yobikō*) or "entrance examination preparatory school" after regular school hours for additional instruction.

The Japanese are obsessed with getting into a prestigious university because it is extremely advantageous for them to establish intimate personal relationships among classmates during their school years. These personal relationships, called *gakubatsu* or "school cliques," are important and permanent interpersonal networks that can be used effectively in both professional and social situations. Without these, it is very difficult for anyone to succeed in Japanese society.

Japanese society functions quite differently from Western societies. It emphasizes vertical interpersonal relationships based on differing ranks and status based on sex, age, rank, and occupation. Typical Japanese interaction tends to move along a scale of respectfulness or rudeness according to the status each person holds. Extreme sensitivity to rank order is often found in a list of coauthors or founders of a new professional association. The list usually includes a sentence that says *Aiueo jun* or "The order of names is alphabetical" or *Junjo fudō* or "No order implied." These statements are to avoid offending anyone on the list by wrong placement of names and to avoid having the readers interpret the list as a hierarchical order. For the same reason, it is a common practice to omit all titles of honor in a list of names. In this case, the list must have a statement that says *Keishō shōryaku* or "Titles of honor are omitted." Respect for status is also shown by using titles of honor such as *sensei* (teacher), *shachō* (president), or *kaichō* (chairman) instead of common honorifics such as Mr., Mrs., or Miss. In some instances, the person's professional title alone is intentionally used without his or her name.

Situational ethics is an important concept in understanding the ethical principles of the Japanese. Unlike the Western ethics of universal ethical principles based on Christianity, Japanese ethical principles are flexible and situational. Basically, the Japanese concept of ethics comes from the Confucian philosophy of filial piety and the Buddhist compassion toward all living beings. It also comes from the idea that both cosmic and human worlds have the division of yan and yin (good and evil, day and night, lightness and darkness, male and female). Since these two opposing forces alternate with and balance each other, there is no strict good and bad or black and white dichotomy. Therefore, the Japanese believe that ethics and morality should be judged relative to social situations.

Social control in Japanese society takes unique forms. *Haji* or "shame before the judgment of society" is the strongest form of social control, and every Japanese is always worried about *gaibun* or "what others talk about." For example, a Japanese mother would scold her child who did not study hard and failed a college entrance examination by saying, "I am so ashamed that you failed the examination. What do you think our relatives, neighbors, and friends will say about you!" The child is made to understand that this failure brings shame to him, every member of his family, his relatives, and even to his teachers and tutors. In extreme cases, students have been known to commit suicide to end the agony of being branded a shameful failure. Two other common social sanctions are *bachi* or "heaven's punishment" and *in'nen* or "karma." The Japanese often say that heaven watches over the deeds of human beings, and it will punish one who commits evil deeds. Many Japanese also believe in the Buddhist concept of karma based on the cosmic principle of rewards and punishments for the acts performed in a previous incarnation. For example, the evil deed done by an ancestor will cause deformity or a strange disease on his descendants a few generations later. In contrast, the good deed done by another ancestor will provide a very happy family life for his great-grandchildren. Westerners may dismiss these matters as superstitions, but many Japanese go to a Shinto shrine or a Buddhist temple to have a priest perform a special service to get rid of their *bachi* or bad karma.

Exchanging personal favors is also an important aspect of social relationships in Japan. Recipients of favors should feel a strong sense of *on* or "debt of gratitude" to those who provide favors. *On* actually refers to a "social credit" from the giver's point of view and to a "social debt" from the receiver's point of view. For example, a professor who taught a student and also found him a good job has earned himself "social credit." On the other hand, the student owes the professor "social debt" for the favors that he has received. *On* is quite different from the Western concept of simply paying back a favor, since Japanese *on* is an "unlimited debt of gratitude" that cannot be easily repaid. *Onjin* or a "benefactor" expects repayment of this social debt for many, many years. In fact, giving *on* to many people can be a "social investment." In contrast, receiving *on* can mean a loss of freedom for the recipient, and he may be burdened with it. This feeling is expressed as *giri* or "sense of obligation." This particular Japanese social custom requires that *on* receivers repay their debts out of the sense of *giri*. One who fails to do so will be called *on-shirazu* or "unaware of social debt" or "ungrateful" and ostracized by the society. Astute Japanese politicians and businessmen often exploit this *on-giri kankei* or "creditor-debtor relationship" to obtain favors and personal gains.

As explained above, Japan has a unique history and geography, a homogeneous population, different political and educational systems, and a hierarchically structured society and culture with complex rules for interpersonal relationships. A good understanding of these factors is absolutely necessary for Western businesspeople in doing business with Japan. This book provides a guide for the businessperson, covering such important topics as barriers to intercultural business communication, the nature of Japanese business organizations, establishing and maintaining business relations, interpersonal communication and sales presentation, contract negotiation, decision making, public speaking and presentations, working for overseas Japanese multinational companies, and living and working in Japan.

c h a p t e r 1

Barriers to Intercultural Business Communication

Two major barriers to effective intercultural communication are
differences in language and in culture. Unless both participants
are truly bilingual and bicultural, they will find communication
very difficult and sometimes frustrating. One of the parties in an
intercultural communication is usually forced to speak a foreign
language. If the foreign language ability of that party is less than
adequate, he or she will be handicapped. In most instances, it is the
Japanese participant who must cope with this handicap because
English, not Japanese, is the most common language of international business. Serious difficulty expressing himself in English will
become a barrier to communication. In addition, if he is not familiar with other cultures, he will routinely use his own Japanese culture as the basis of perception and understanding.

Americans routinely complain about certain Japanese
communication habits: (1) The Japanese are so polite and so cautious that you never know what they are thinking. They do not say
anything and keep on nodding smilingly as if they are agreeing,
even when they have doubts and disagreements. (2) The Japanese
use vague words and ambiguous expressions and expect others to
draw conclusions. (3) The Japanese are too formal and seem to
always weigh the meaning of this or that. (4) The Japanese are
notoriously slow in making decisions and always avoid making
quick and spontaneous decisions. (5) The Japanese are always apologizing, even when there seems to be nothing to apologize for.
(6) The Japanese use silence when they wish to avoid a direct
answer.[1]

These distinctively Japanese communication behaviors have apparently been influenced by the nature of the Japanese language, by common Japanese communication habits in interpersonal communication interactions, and by such Japanese cultural variables as beliefs, values, attitudes, self-perception, social organization, nonverbal gestures and postures, use of space, and concept of time. To eliminate barriers of communication with the Japanese, it is absolutely necessary to understand these important linguistic and cultural variables.

Linguistic Barriers to Communication

Japanese is considered one of the most complicated languages. It has three different ways of writing: *kanji* (Chinese characters), *hiragana* (alphabet), and *katakana* (a different alphabet). The Japanese must learn to read and write more than 3,000 *kanji* characters and their combinations, *hiragana*, and *katakana* as well. And because the Japanese language does not belong to the Indo-European family of languages, its pronunciation and syntax are quite different from those of Western languages. Thousands of English loan words are also included in Japanese vocabulary, but the pronunciation of these words is radically modified in accordance with the unique Japanese phonetic system.

Language is a self-contained system and the most appropriate expression of the culture in which it is used. Every language has its own unique vocabulary, idioms, and cultural expressions.

The Nature of Japanese Language

Japanese language has only five vowels and seventeen consonant phonemes. The vowels are either short or long. Every consonant, except one [n], is always followed by one of the five vowels. Accent and intonation patterns are very different from those in English. The basic sentence structure of a sentence is subject-object-verb. For example, "This is a dictionary" is arranged "This *(Kore)* dictionary *(jisho)* is *(desu)*." Noun-verb agreement is not important, because the same verb form, *desu*, can be used for singular or plural objects. Quite often the subject is dropped as it is in Spanish. In addition, there are no equivalents of the English articles "a" and "the" in Japanese.

Because of these differences, Japanese when speaking in English mispronounce certain words and make grammatical mistakes. Native speakers of Japanese cannot distinguish between [l] and [r] sounds when hearing them. For example, they cannot tell the difference between these two sounds in the pairs of words such as "light" and "right," "club" and "crab," and "lice" and "rice" when they hear them. And when they speak, they usually substitute English [l] and [r] with the Japanese [r] or "flapped r," which sounds somewhere between [r] and [l]. Other sounds that do not exist in Japanese are consonant sounds such as [f] (as in fox), [v] (as in vase), [th] (as in that), [sh] (as in ship), [ch] (as in chart), [wh] (as in where), and vowel sounds such as [a] (as in cat), [ə] (as in sun), [ó] (as in ought), and [e] as in egg). Because the Japanese language does not have consonant clusters as English does, the word "street" may be pronounced as "sutoriito" with a vowel after each consonant.

The Japanese may also omit articles, ignore noun–verb agreement, and fail to use proper English accent and intonation. Unfortunately, Japanese-accented English with grammatical mistakes can become a serious barrier to communication.

Another important feature of the Japanese language is that it is extremely status-oriented because Japan is a hierarchical society. For example, there are several different pronouns for "you" in Japanese: *sochira, otaku, anata, kimi, omae,* and *temē* in order of politeness. The most common pronoun, *anata,* can never be used when talking to a person of higher status. Verb usage is also influenced by relative social status. For example, the English word "come" can be translated as *omie ni narimasu, oide ni narimasu, irrasshaimasu, kimasu,* or *kuru.* Every Japanese is expected to know how he or she should speak depending on the situation. Americans from an egalitarian society will be confused and frustrated if they have to learn and speak in Japanese according to these rules.

Still one more source of confusion in Japanese-American communication is how questions are answered. In the Japanese language, it is grammatically correct to say "Yes, I don't agree with you" in response to the question "You don't agree with me, do you?" This problem of communication is often amplified by the habitual use of *hai* or "yes." Japanese frequently say *Hai, wakari-*

mashita or "Yes, I understand" when they hear something being said, but this may simply mean "Yes, I hear what you are saying." It may not necessarily mean "Yes. I agree with you." In many instances, Japanese may unconsciously transfer this particular Japanese communication habit into situations when they are speaking in English. This leads to the common complaint by American businesspeople that the Japanese frequently say "yes" when they mean "no."

Imai explains that it is not in the Japanese tradition to "call a spade a spade." The most typical way that the Japanese imply "no" is to say "yes" and then to follow this with an explanation that may last half an hour. They use window-dressing interjections such as "But of course," "By all means," or "Quite right" in the affirmative tone. The second way is to be so vague, ambiguous, and evasive in reply that the other side loses track of what the issue was. The third way is simply not to answer the question and to leave the matter unattended. Other ways of implying "no" include abruptly changing the subject, criticizing the other party, or suddenly assuming a highly apologetic tone.[2] To achieve successful communication, both the Japanese and their English-speaking counterparts need to understand whose cultural interpretation is being used when they try to interpret each other's message.

Common Japanese Habits in Interpersonal Communication Interactions

In Western cultures, a conversation or dialogue involves two people, a speaker and a listener, who exchange words like balls in a Ping-Pong game. But the Japanese do not carry on a conversation in this way; they are not expected "to produce a conversation jointly." More specifically, they give each other *aizuchi* or "agreeable responses" that make a conversation go smoothly. These responses are *hai* (yes), *ee* (yes: informal), *haa* (yes: formal), *sō* (that's right), *sō-da* (that's it, that's it exactly), and *naruhodo nee* (indeed). *Aizuchi* also includes nonverbal affirmative responses like nodding and smiling. The giving of this *aizuchi*, however, does not mean that the listener really understands or agrees with the content of an utterance. It simply means "Yes, I am listening to what you are saying. Please go on."[3] This habitual use of *aizuchi* by the Japanese can cause certain communication problems when they are speaking in English. For example, an American businessman, Mr. Smith, is talking about a business deal to be consummated with his Japanese counterpart, Mr. Kato. Their dialogue may go as follows:

Smith: "Regarding the proposed contract . . . "

Kato: "Yes, yes. . . "

Smith: "You don't see any problems . . . "

Kato: "That's right . . . "

Smith: "All the terms and conditions . . . "

Kato: "Yes, indeed . . . "

Smith: "Then, can we sign it this morning, and . . . "

Kato: "Yes, but big problems, you know . . ."

Smith: "I thought you were saying that everything was okay! What do you mean you have problems now?"

13

Mr. Smith was first annoyed by interruptions by Mr. Kato, then he misunderstood those seemingly affirmative responses, and finally, he became upset when he found out that those "yeses" were simply *aizuchi* or mere recognition of what was being said. For Mr. Kato, however, this was a normal pattern of dialogue.

Since the Japanese are extremely concerned about interpersonal harmony and protection of each other's "face" in face-to-face encounters, they use a variety of ingenious tactics of interpersonal communication. Some of these tactics are "anticipatory communication," "self-communication," "understatement," and "acting as delegate."[4] "Anticipatory communication" is a communication tactic in which the speaker expects the listener or the third party to anticipate his wish, without having to ask for what he wants. The listener is expected to guess and accommodate the speaker's needs, sparing him of any possible embarrassment. For example, when a nearly bankrupt businessman is visiting a bank loan officer, he does not ask for a loan directly but talks about the severe worldwide recession. He will walk away empty-handed unless the loan officer volunteers to help him with a loan. Thus, both of them can spare embarrassment and loss of face.

In "self-communication," the speaker mumbles something to himself, expecting others around him to hear what he has said. The listeners, then, either acknowledge it or pretend they did not hear anything. Unless someone is willing to recognize his message and help him, the speaker can deny that he said anything. For example, the speaker mumbles loud enough, "This room is too cold," instead of asking someone to adjust the thermostat.

"Understatement" is a device to avoid making an assertive and irreversible statement. The Japanese language allows subtle and open-ended understatements because syntactically it is not necessary to state the subject, and the verb of negation or affirmation comes at the end of a sentence. For example, a Japanese businessman can say, "This breach of contract . . . ," and stop and wait for a listener's reaction before going on to complete his statement after hearing the listener's reaction. If the listener becomes very angry, he might say, "I agree with you. This breach of contract is a serious matter and we should address it immediately." But if the listener does not seem too upset, he could change his conclusion and say, "I thought it wouldn't be a major problem with you."

"Acting as delegate" is another common tactic in which the speaker conveys his own message as being that of someone else. He would say, "I personally don't care, but my supervisor will never allow this," when his supervisor is not concerned about it all.

Cultural Barriers to Effective Communication

Culture is the software of the human mind that provides an operating environment for human behavior, and all members within the same environment share important characteristics of the culture.[5] Every human being acquires his culture through years of socialization processes from family members, other members of society, and the mass media. Culture will have a strong influence on the individual's perception, communication behavior, and physical activities. The culture teaches appropriate ways of living and of interacting with others. Cultural knowledge includes experiences, beliefs, values, attitudes, meanings, hierarchies, religion, self-concept, role expectations, use of space, concept of time, and material objects.

In business communication, for example, Japanese business-men use standards of Japanese business ethics, Japanese business practices and conventions, Japanese social and cultural values, stereotypical images of foreign businessmen, and secondhand information on how business is done in certain foreign countries.[6] To overcome cultural barriers of communication with the Japanese, Westerners need to understand several critical Japanese cultural variables and their relationship to intercultural communication.

World View and Patterns of Thought

The way people view their own physical and spiritual world is a function of their culture. The traditional Japanese view of the world, that a person must maintain a harmonious relationship with nature, is derived from both Shinto and Buddhist beliefs. The world is spiritual and organic, and it operates in a mystically ordered and spiritually conceivable manner. All living things such as animals, fishes, insects, trees, and plants, and inanimate objects such as mountains, rivers, rocks, earth, rivers, lakes, and oceans have spirits. Despite recent modernization and technological advancements in Japan, this world view has not been changed drastically. The Japanese are still superstitious and try to maintain harmony with spiritual and supernatural forces.

The ordinary Japanese household has *kamidana* (small Shinto shrine) for its guardian gods and *butsudan* (small Buddhist altar) for the family's ancestors. It is common for a modern sky-scraper to have a Shinto shrine for the god of its building site on the rooftop or in a rock garden. Before leveling off a mountain for highway construction, a Japanese construction company will ask a Shinto priest to hold a special prayer service and dedicate offerings to appease the spirit of the mountain. Medical schools hold a monthly *dōbutsu kuyō* (Buddhist funeral service for animals) to comfort the souls of the experimental animals sacrificed in the pre-ceding month. This service is attended by members of the faculty and the research staff.

Many Japanese still plan certain events or activities based on old superstitions. Days designated by the old Chinese calendar for happy events and for unhappy events are still observed. For example, *tomobiki* and *taian* are good days for weddings, signing

15

contracts, ground-breaking ceremonies or dedicating a new building. *Butsumetsu* is a very bad day for such happy events, but it is a suitable day for a funeral. Four and nine are bad numbers because their pronunciations in Japanese, *shi* and *ku,* are homonyms for "death" and "suffering." Japanese hospitals do not have Room 4 or Room 9. The lucky numbers are three, five, and seven, and gifts are given in these odd numbers.

Concept of Self and Role Expectations

The Japanese person is concerned about himself primarily in his relationship to his group because his group affiliations are extremely important in Japanese culture. Every Japanese must also learn his "proper place" in a social group, institution, or society as a whole. His self-identify is not an individual identity separate from his family, relatives, school or workplace, or society; rather, it is the fraction that he is allowed to occupy as a member of these groups he belongs to. He is expected to play a specific role or roles according to his prescribed social and occupational positions. A father is expected to work diligently as the breadwinner. A mother is expected to become a full-time homemaker and to devote herself to the housework and caring for her husband and children instead of becoming a career woman.

In Japanese society, one's proper position or status is determined by one's position in a hierarchical structure. The Japanese differentiate ranks of *sempai* (senior) and *kohai* (junior) by the slightest difference in age, graduation time, the time of entry into a company, and so on. *Sempai* is expected to take care of *kohai,* and in turn, *kohai* must respect *sempai* and be willing to do anything for him. For example, in a high school tennis practice, a junior player always acts as ball boy (or water boy) and watches a senior's play. He may not be allowed to play in a tournament, even if he is better than the senior player.

Ethnocentrism and Nationalistic Mentality

Ethnocentrism is the tendency to evaluate other ethnic groups by using one's own group and culture as the standard for all judgments. The members of a certain ethnic group consider themselves superior to others because they believe that they are the best and that their ways are the only correct ways. Ethnocentrism comes from the feeling of superiority and blind belief in their own racial characteristics and their political system, politics, economic system, education system, religion, morality, and social customs.[7]

The Japanese have a very strong ethnocentric attitude. They believe that their culture is unique and superior to that of other countries, even though they have borrowed so much from other cultures. They feel that they are of a superior race despite the fact that their ancestors came from China, Korea, Mongolia, the Malay Peninsula, and other Asian countries. They are extremely nationalistic when it comes to doing business with foreigners. For Japanese politicians and businessmen, national interests have always been the highest priority in diplomacy and in international trade. They tend to see "appropriateness" or "fairness" of their actions only from the standpoint of Japan's own national interests. They are very slow in responding to *gaiatsu* or "foreign pressure," especially on trade issues, if it will hurt any of the important domestic industries.

Americans are even more ethnocentric because they know that the United States has been the major economic and military superpower of the world. They also firmly believe that American democratic ideals and social values are superior to those of other countries. Many American political leaders still seem to believe rather naively that "Americanization" is the key to solving all international conflicts, whatever they may be. In Japan-U.S. trade relations, Americans have been urging the Japanese "not to behave like Japanese any more" but follow American ways. For example, Malcolm Baldrige, former secretary of the U.S. Department of Commerce, declared that "because 'cultural traditions' were a major cause of their bilateral trade surplus, they simply have to be changed. . . . Japan now has the second largest economy in the free world."[8] For American politicians, "Japan bashing" was an effective way to gain votes from American constituents who were threatened by the so-called Japanese economic invasion of the late 1980s.

Differences in Cultural Values

All cultures have traditional values or frames of reference that provide people with a set of rules or norms. Cultural values have

17

become the basis upon which people judge their own behavior and the behavior of others. These values define what is good and bad, true and false, positive and negative. When people holding different cultural values try to communicate with each other, the differences in value orientations can cause inaccurate judgments and serious breakdowns in communication. Desirable values in one culture can be negative values in another. To minimize possible communication breakdowns, all contrasting cultural values should be analyzed and explained. Several important contrasting Japanese and American cultural values are as follows:

Hierarchy vs. Egalitarianism

The Japanese have a strong desire to know each other's relative social status by age, time of graduation, the year of entering a company, and the rank of institutions with which a person is affiliated. They need to recognize the ranks along a vertical social scale before they can freely engage in interpersonal communication. When they meet for the first time, they routinely ask direct or indirect questions to obtain status-related information. Then, they will choose proper forms of address and the appropriate level of polite language. In contrast, Americans have a strong tendency to dismiss status differences and talk to one another on equal terms. Americans feel more comfortable in calling each other by their first names. Japanese, however, feel uncomfortable if they are addressed by their first name.

Group Orientation vs. Individualism

Japan is a group-oriented society in which every person belongs to a group or groups. His affiliation with a certain group gives him a social identity, support, and protection. If he wishes to succeed in life, he is expected to live and work as a group member, not as an independent individual. The Japanese are conditioned to act together from a very early age. Preschool children engage in group play, and school children study and play sports in groups and travel in groups with their classmates. In high school and in college, students join clubs and circles to nurture group spirit and comradeship. When they graduate and join a work group, they are expected to follow the wishes of that group. The legendary "rugged individualism" of American culture is not only unacceptable, but is regarded as "egotistic" and "selfish" in the Japanese cultural context.

Harmony vs. Aggressiveness

Harmony *(wa)* is one of the most important Japanese cultural values. The Japanese believe that harmonious interpersonal relationships should be maintained at all costs. They avoid displaying overt aggressiveness or disruptive attitudes in public. Interpersonal conflicts or confrontations are embarrassing to them. In contrast, Americans generally accept aggression as fun and constructive, and they often take an aggressive give-and-take as a kind of game.

Conformity vs. Defiance

The stress on harmony and consensus generates social pressures for conformity on the Japanese. From an early age, Japanese children are not only conditioned to conform to the hierarchical pressures from their family members, teachers, and school administrators, but also to the horizontal pressures of their schoolmates. When they become adults and join work groups, they are again pressured to conform to group norms. Because the sense of their identity is anchored in group affiliation, they suppress their desire to be different or conspicuous in order to avoid being rejected. Consequently, they generally choose conformity rather than defiance whenever they are forced to make individual choices, and they will refrain from expressing disagreement with whatever appears to be the majority's opinion. This self-restraint is called *enryo*, which is considered an important social virtue frequently displayed in social interactions by the Japanese.[9] To the Japanese, social conformity is not a sign of being a weak-willed yes-man, but the product of inner strength and self-discipline.[10]

Emotionalism vs. Rationality

The Japanese are generally more emotional and subjective than Americans in their interactions with other people. They make important decisions based on emotions and subjective judgment of people and situations rather than on objective data and information. For example, instead of trying to get the best price through open bidding, a Japanese businessman may decide to continue a business relationship with a supplier only because he is an old friend. In fact, many Japanese companies maintain business relationships based on emotional ties between old friends and associates rather than on purely rational and objective contractual ties. On the other hand, American businessmen tend to be more rational and calculating in their business dealings with each other, even though some Americans may behave like Japanese. Americans are much more willing to separate business from friendship when they need to make a choice.

Face-saving vs. Pragmatism

Face-saving is extremely important for every Japanese. Japanese government leaders, businessmen, educators, family heads, and even gangsters take certain actions just to save face. Japanese diplomats have often been criticized for engaging in geisha diplomacy or *happō bijin gaikō* or "looking-beautiful-for-everyone diplomacy." For example, former prime minister Yasuhiro Nakasone went to Baghdad on an unofficial mission and used "friendly persuasion" on Saddam Hussein to try to get him to withdraw his troops from Kuwait. Subsequently, the Japanese government donated $13 billion to the United States to support the Gulf War. It seemed that the government sent him as an "unofficial emissary" to make Japan look good in the eyes of the Arab world, but Japan also took sides with the Western nations by providing a financial contribution. A food caterer in Nagoya will use a Toyota van to deliver lunches to a Toyota car dealer and a Nissan pickup truck to make the delivery to a Nissan dealership.

Sensitivity to "face" can be illustrated with several commonly used expressions: *kao ni doro wo nuru* (having face smeared with mud); *kao wo tsubushu* (having face crushed); *kao ga tatanai* (face not honored); *kao ga kiku* (having an effective face); *kao ga hiroi* (having a widely recognized face). For example, when a college student obtains a good job through the influence of his professor, he cannot resign from this position because he would be smearing the professor's face with mud. Or a daughter may go through an arranged marriage and stay in an unhappy marriage in order not to dishonor the face of the go-between who happens to be her father's immediate superior. In many instances, the Japanese are not pragmatic and realistic when it comes to face-saving.

Conservatism vs. Social Mobility

The Japanese are far more conservative and concerned with maintaining the status quo than Americans are. They are more reluctant to make any changes that may disrupt harmonious interpersonal relationships, although they are more willing to adopt technological changes. For example, when a Japanese company purchases new machine tools, it may hire a few young and competent engineers to assist the older managers who are no longer productive instead of simply laying off the older managers.

New high school and college graduates expect to work for the same company for their entire working life. They will not look for better-paying jobs with another company because they prefer job security to the challenge of a new opportunity. Intercompany mobility is discouraged, and most Japanese companies are not willing to hire midcareer transferees from other companies.

The Japanese still respect and retain old social customs and rituals that Western observers consider no longer necessary. For example, Japanese businessmen send *nengajō* (new year's greeting cards) to their important clients and also make a courtesy call to thank them for the past year's patronage and ask for their continued patronage in the new year. Japanese businesses buy talismans and other lucky charms from certain Shinto shrines that are believed to bring good luck and abundance of profits when they could use computer simulations to make more-accurate forecasts.

Acquiescence vs. Rejection of Authority

Since the Japanese have lived in a hierarchical society for centuries, they are conditioned to acquiesce to pressures from authority. In the feudal days of the Tokugawa era, farmers and commoners had to unconditionally obey samurai lords because defiance meant instant death. At the time of the Meiji Restoration of 1868, and again immediately after Japan's defeat in World War II, the Japanese government and its bureaucrats took control and guided industries in rebuilding Japan. Even today, government bureaucrats and school authorities still retain their traditional power over the daily lives of Japanese citizens. Ordinary Japanese do not even dream of rejecting these authorities. This submissive behavior of the Japanese derives from the ancient Confucius teaching and traditional hier-

21

archical relationships between government officials and average citizens. A Japanese citizen knows that any overt defiance or action against authority will result in official or "unofficial" punishments. If a disgruntled parent openly protests a school authority's handling of his son, the school will make it extremely unpleasant for the son to stay on. Suddenly, the child may lose all his good friends and teachers' support, no matter how legitimate the parent's complaint might have been. In many such cases, this child will suffer from *ijime* (cruel bullying) from his classmates and even from teachers.[11] Acquiescence indeed makes things go smoothly in Japan because rejection of authority can cause unpleasant consequences. In short, deference to authority is an important value in Japanese culture.

22

Differences in Nonverbal Communication Behavior

It is a commonly held misconception that if people cannot communicate with foreigners through spoken language, they should resort to gestures and body language. Most people undoubtedly believe that nonverbal behaviors are the same or at least very similar across cultures, but this is an erroneous assumption. Many nonverbal behaviors from different cultures carry different meanings. In fact, certain Japanese facial expressions, gestures, and body movements communicate entirely different meanings and cause misunderstandings. The following explanations deal with specific differences in nonverbal behaviors of Japanese and Americans:

Facial Expressions

The so-called Japanese smile has often been a subject of discussion among Western businesspeople. Westerners generally interpret laughing and smiling as signs of happiness, joy, or agreement, but the Japanese may also "smile" when they feel embarrassed and "laugh" when they want to hide their anger. For example, when a Japanese salesclerk makes a mistake, she may "smilingly" apologize to a customer. A Japanese businessman may "laugh it off" when he smashes his new Mercedes Benz in a traffic accident, even though he really feels very angry with himself. Or a Japanese buyer may say, "I just cannot do business with you this time," with a big smile and offer no further explanation.

In similar situations, an American salesperson will have a "long face" as she apologizes. A very irate American motorist may show his anger openly by shouting obscene words. An American buyer will look at his business associate and, without a smile, explain why he cannot do business with him this time.

The Japanese do not show "honest facial expressions" because Japanese culture emphasizes self-control over the public display of emotions. They even show "put-on smiles" for public display when they are not in a happy mood. Indeed, it is easy for Westerners to misinterpret the Japanese "smile" and "laughter" as insincere, dishonest, or even mocking. The myth of the "inscrutable Japanese" no doubt has its roots in these misinterpretations. A popular Japanese management consultant advises, "Never take 'yes' for an answer. Don't take a smile for 'yes,' when doing business with the Japanese."[12]

Eye Contact

There is a bit of a "culture clash" between Japanese and Americans in interpretation of eye contact. In the dominant white-American culture, sustained direct eye contact usually means interest, honesty, sincerity, and positive attitude. The avoidance of eye contact or shifting of the eyes usually means lack of interest, dishonesty, slyness, and negative attitude. In Japanese culture, however, direct eye contact means aggression, rudeness, insistence of equality, and even belligerence. For example, a Japanese college student shows respect by not looking at the eyes of his professor. In contrast, an American student maintains good eye contact with his professor for the same reason. A Japanese businessman frequently shifts his eyes during a difficult negotiation session because he feels that sustained eye contact might be overbearing and rude. But this shifting of the eyes may well be interpreted by his American business associate as an indication of dishonesty or disinterest. A Japanese teenager who looks his father in the eye while being scolded will be punished more severely, because the direct eye contact with his father means that he is being belligerent and disrespectful. In contrast, an American parent insists that his teenage son look him in the eye. This is an extension of the Western belief that one cannot tell a lie while looking directly at an authority figure.

Gestures, Body Movement, and Postures

Several frequently used Japanese gestures carry different meanings in other cultures. The hand gesture of beckoning with an open hand with a palm down means "come here" in Japan, but it is similar to the American gesture of "good-bye." Pointing at the nose with the index finger means "me," in Japan, but it may be simply "nose" in American culture. Moving the open hand back and forth in front of the face as if fanning means "no" or "no, thank you" in Japan. To Americans, it may look like chasing bugs or fanning one's face.

The Japanese tend to move about quickly, with short strides and drooping shoulders. To Americans, who tend to walk in longer strikes and with a more upright posture, the Japanese may appear insecure and unmotivated.

The Japanese low posture *(teishisei)* is perhaps the most confusing of all Japanese nonverbal behaviors. *Atama ga hikui* or "one's head is low" posture is a desirable demonstration of humility frequently displayed in public by the Japanese, especially when they are greeting a person of higher status. To Westerners, this low posture looks like a sign of weakness or lack of confidence rather than deference.

Physical Appearance and Attire

Even though young Japanese are getting taller, the Japanese are generally much shorter than Westerners. The stereotype of a typical Japanese businessman wearing a dark blue or gray striped suit, a white shirt, an expensive brand-name tie, and a Swiss watch and carrying a Canon camera is not entirely without substance. Although many American companies have somewhat casual dress policies, Japanese business attire continues to be formal and status oriented. The Japanese are also inclined to show off their professional status or wealth with objects that they wear. A top Japanese executive might wear a gold Rolex watch; Dunhill necktie pin, cufflinks, and belt buckle; tailor-made Armani suit; Ferragamo shoes; and Christian Dior gold-rim glasses while showing off his Cartier gold ball-point pen.

The Japanese always pay close attention to what every person is wearing, especially when they meet a group of people for the first time. A businessman with badly coordinated attire cannot create a favorable first impression. When dealing with the Japanese,

Western businesspeople need to remember that wearing casual or sporty attire may create an unfavorable impression.

Interpersonal Space

Every culture prescribes how people should use and organize space between people. It also assigns meanings to various personal distances. Every individual learns the appropriate interpersonal distance defined by his culture for each of a variety of social interactions. He will feel uncomfortable or threatened when his space is violated, even unintentionally.

Although there are no research findings on social distances for Japanese people, it appears that the Japanese, especially those who live and work in overcrowded urban centers, cannot maintain personal distances that Westerners consider desirable. Not only have the Japanese learned to maximize the use of small physical spaces, but they have also learned to use nonverbal cues such as changing their posture or body position and avoiding eye contact to compensate for the discomfort caused by smaller personal territories. Bowing distance is wider than hand-shaking distance, but when they bow to each other in a small space, they stand sideways to avoid bumping heads. In a very crowded train packed with commuters, Japanese men cross their arms in front and women hold up their handbags or shopping bags between themselves and strangers. To avoid eye contact, they try to stand shoulder to shoulder and never face each other. The Japanese rarely apologize to each other when they bump into or step on each other in a crowded train. Perhaps they do not want to recognize others' presence by acknowledging the unintended mishaps. In a very busy restaurant, total strangers are routinely seated face to face at the same table with their consent. This sharing of a table is called *aiseki*. Since Japanese are used to living in crowded conditions, they can tolerate this invasion of personal space with little difficulty.

Arrangement of Furniture and Personal Space

The arrangement of furniture in an office or a home also determines interpersonal space between people who use them. A typical Japanese office is cluttered with many small desks in several rows. Each desk has a telephone, a small desktop computer, and a file tray. There are no partitions in front and between these desks. Office workers sit on both sides facing each other. A section chief occupies a slightly larger desk in one corner of the open room. From his desk, he can oversee what is going on in the office. He may have a small upholstered chair and a coffee table next to his desk. In this office layout, telephone conversations and other communication can easily be shared among co-workers sitting nearby, and the manager can also monitor whatever business matters are being handled. He may even volunteer to assist his subordinates, if he feels that he should step in. Because of this arrangement of physical space, interpersonal communication among Japanese co-workers and supervisors is instantaneous and involuntary at times. Because of its lack of privacy, Westerners, especially individualistic Americans, might find this Japanese office arrangement very uncomfortable and annoying.

The seating arrangement at a conference table is another important aspect of Japanese corporate culture because it determines proper personal distances between participants. The seating arrangement represents the hierarchical structure or status relationships of all members who are present. For example, the highest-ranking person sits at the head of the conference table; those of lower status sit away from him in a descending order. Violation of this protocol of seating will create uneasiness and discomfort among the Japanese participants attending a conference.

Tactile Communication

Touching is one of the most sensitive of all forms of communication in interpersonal interactions. In Western culture, commonly used forms of tactile communication are patting, slapping, punching, pinching, stroking, shaking, kissing, holding, embracing, grooming, and tickling. The rules of touching in Japanese culture are quite different, and the same forms may have different meanings.

Touching is the first form of communication that humans experience. Parents express affection to newborn babies by cuddling, patting, feeling, nuzzling, and kissing. Soon the babies begin to imitate their parents; and by the time they reach adulthood, they will have acquired a wide range of tactile communication behavior. In every culture, new members are being taught a large number of specific methods of tactile communication that are considered appropriate in various social contexts. Japanese mothers tend to have more frequent and intimate body contact with their infants than do Western mothers. They still breast-feed for several months, and mothers and infants sleep in the same bedroom until the babies are a year old. They also co-bathe in the deep Japanese-style bathtub *(furo)* at home. Thus, Japanese mothers and infants share the pleasures of nursing and bathing, and they communicate affection to each other through body contact rather than through verbal means.[13] A mother also carries her baby on her back when doing house chores and when shopping.

As the children grow older, Japanese parents have much less tactile communication with their children. Japanese teenagers avoid being "babied" (touched) by their parents in public. Japanese teenage boys, especially, feel very embarrassed if their mothers touch them in front of their friends because they are expected to show independence or manliness at an earlier age than teenage girls. Japanese parents do not show affection by hugging and kissing in front of their children, and even Japanese honeymooners hesitate to hug and kiss in public.

One aspect of Japanese tactile communication that often confounds Weterners is that young Japanese women often hold hands and walk around. They even go to discos and dance together. Male students and young adults may also walk together, arms around each other's shoulders. This form of tactile communication by the Japanese makes Americans uncomfortable, as this behavior is often associated with homosexuality in Western culture.

Social kissing, a common means of American tactile communication, is still embarrassing to the Japanese. It is interesting to see Japanese visitors to Hawai'i who look embarrassed and blush upon receiving kisses and hugs given by lei greeters at Hawaiian hula shows. To many Japanese men, the gesture signals "erotic intimacy."

Shaking hands, another common method of greeting in Western countries, has been adopted by the Japanese in recent years. However, their handshakes have been modified by the Japanese custom of bowing. Japanese people have a strong tendency to shake hands and bow at the same time, thereby failing to maintain good eye contact. They also tend to hold the other's hand a little too long because they are accustomed to keeping on bowing for a few minutes, mumbling words of gratitude or greetings. Some Japanese women use both hands to hold the other person's hand and keep on talking for a while.

Time Usage

Time is another important variable, because how time is used communicates meaning. In both Japanese and Western cultures, punctuality communicates respect, and tardiness is an insult. In a highly industrialized society, time is treated as a "tangible commodity." In the American business culture, time is handled as if it were a long loaf of bread that can be sliced up and sold in slices separately. A desk calendar used by American businessmen has eighteen lines indicating 30-minute intervals of time from 8:00 A.M. to 5:00 P.M. A large percentage of American workers get paid hourly wages. Even professionals such as lawyers and public accountants calculate their fees on the number of hours needed for a particular case or accounting job.

In comparison, Japanese businesspeople cannot handle time strictly as a tangible commodity, even though they are just as time conscious as Westerners. Because the time usage in Japan is usually determined by the status relationships between the people involved, Japanese businesspeople must use "people-oriented time." A top Japanese executive can have a young management trainee wait for an hour or more without giving him a legitimate excuse. A Japanese salesman making a sales call is almost always made to wait. A retail shopclerk will graciously wait on a demanding customer who hops in only a few minutes before the closing time. A Japanese manager with another appointment waiting may hesitate to cut off a social conversation with a very important visitor who has overstayed. This mode of time usage often angers Westerners, who take appointments and deadlines seriously. To avoid frustrations and misunderstanding, it is important to learn how the Japanese use time in a variety of specific social situations.

Government–Business Relationship and Business Organizations in Japan

Japanese business organizations are quite different from those in the West. Many of the major Japanese industries were started by the government shortly after the Meiji Restoration of 1868. Even today, they are directly or indirectly controlled by the government ministries and bureaucratic elites. Unlike the adversarial relationship often found in the United States, the government-business relationship in Japan is one of close collaboration. This close tie is referred to as "Japan, Incorporated" by many American politicians and business leaders. They charge that Japan behaves like a huge conglomerate in which the Japanese government, particularly the Ministry of International Trade and Industry (MITI), functions as the corporate headquarters, and that each enterprise is a branch or division of the corporation.[1] Western observers believe that bureaucratic elites in key Japanese ministries exercise virtually total control over Japanese business enterprises through close collaboration and cooperation. Westerners also believe that many Japanese industries are controlled by a handful of major conglomerates called *keiretsu*.

Despite the recent push for liberalization and deregulation of the Japanese economy, government bureaucrats and big businesses continue to exert their power and influence over the running of Japan. Open and free competition among individual enterprises still does not exist in Japan as it does in the West. Westerners, therefore, must understand the particular government-business relationship in Japan and the culture of Japanese business organizations when they communicate with Japanese businesspeople.

Powerful Ministries and Bureaucrats

"At the top of Japan's close-knit, homogeneous hierarchy are the greatest ministries of its government and the officials who run them. By cultural heritage, education, attitudes, status, and influence, these men are spiritual heirs of the old Chinese mandarins. They are of key importance in the Japanese government.[2] All Japanese ministries are staffed with elite bureaucrats who provide strong leadership and guidance for every sector of Japanese industry. For example, MITI spells out its "Vision of MITI Policies," which is MITI's blueprint for economic development over a specified time period. Its aim is to attain a specific economic order or economic structure favorable to the national interest. MITI also chooses which industry should be vigorously promoted and which industry should be gradually phased out to maintain Japan's comparative advantage against other industrialized nations. (This process is called "rationalization" of industries.) Directives from MITI, called *gyōsei shidō* or "administrative guidance," are followed by every industry with little defiance or resistance. To reactivate certain depressed industries, MITI often restrains "excessive" competition in both domestic and international trade. Although Japan has its Fair Trade Commission and antitrust laws, the government frequently allows the establishment of legal cartels under which companies may engage in such collaborative activity as joint restrictions on production and joint reduction of capacity. The government's support has always been the most important shield all Japanese industries have had against foreign competition. Another powerful ministry is the Ministry of Finance, which oversees banking, the stock exchange, and other financial activities.

The relationship between elite bureaucrats and private industries is further strengthened through a practice of industry's hiring of retired bureaucrats called *amakudari*. Today, bureaucrats usually retire at 55 years of age, and upon retirement, they "go down" to private-sector companies that they had previously guided. They will be employed as executives or managers in sections or departments of private companies where they can continue to contribute by using their technical knowledge and expertise and the valuable personal relationships they have established over many years of government service. In some instances, these former government regulators go to work for the industries they once regulated. This is another important reason why Japan is able to maintain a smooth and collaborative government-business relationship unlike that in the United States and other Western countries.

Keiretsu or Japan's Business Conglomerates

Japan's *keiretsu* groups have their origins in the *zaibatsu* groups that existed before the end of World War II. The word *zaibatsu* literally means "financial clique," and they were groups of various companies directly controlled by a family holding company. The most famous *zaibatsu* groups were Mitsubishi, Mitsui, Sumitomo, and Yasuda. These *zaibatsu* groups, which aided Japan's military efforts through production of weapons, ships, tanks, airplanes, and other instruments of warfare, were abolished by directive of the Supreme Commander for the Allied Occupation Powers immediately after the end of World War II.[3]

31

However, in 1952, immediately after the end of the occupation, the Japanese government canceled the ban on cross-shareholdings and interlocking boards of directors. The powerful industrial groups were quickly reassembled in a new form called *keiretsu*. The new groups were based on major banks and trading companies that formed networks of companies. These alliances were linked by cross-shareholdings, common bank affiliations, and the use of the same trading company to procure raw materials and to distribute products. Today, there are six major groups: Mitsubishi, Mitsui, Sumitomo, Sanwa, Fuyo, and Dai Ichi Kangyo. Each of these groups has companies in each major sector of the Japanese economy such as steel, petrochemicals, banking, and high technology. In addition, several new groups such as Toyota, Hitachi, Matsushita, Seibu, Tokyu, and Daiei have come into existence since the war.

The two most common classifications of Japanese industrial groups are horizontal *keiretsu* and vertical (or pyramid) *keiretsu*. A horizontal *keiretsu* is a diverse group of companies with different lines of business and an affiliation with the main bank. For example, the Mitsubishi Group is a horizontal *keiretsu* that includes Mitsubishi Bank, Mitsubishi Trust and Banking, Mitsubishi Motors, Mitsubishi Electrics, Mitsubishi Heavy Industry,

Mitsubishi Real Estate, Mitsubishi Trading Company, Meiji Mutual Life and Insurance, Tokio Marine and Fire Insurance, and many other major companies.[4]

A vertical or pyramid *keiretsu* is a cluster of firms linked through the supply and distribution of a principal manufacturer. For example, Toyota Motors is a vertical *keiretsu* with many parts suppliers and dealers that deal either exclusively or principally with Toyota. The parent company owns large blocks of shares in the companies belonging to Toyota Group and provides technical assistance and key managerial talent if necessary. Japan Airlines, a flagship Japanese carrier, is also a vertical *keiretsu;* it includes Japan Air Charter, Japan Asia Airways, JAL Hotel System, JAL Trading, JAL-PAK, Pacifico Creative Tours, International In-Flight Catering Company, and other service companies. The JAL group handles all aspects of international travelers who fly Japan Airlines to destinations all over the world. Japanese manufactures of other automobiles and of electronics also form this type of *keiretsu*.

Japan's trading partners have severely criticized the secretive and exclusive ways of conducting business practiced by Japanese *keiretsu* groups. The U.S. government and businesses have been the most severe critics of these practices, because the whole concept of preferential relationships among group member companies is alien to the American tradition of fair play and open competition.

Japanese Business Organization

A typical Japanese business organization is like a huge family with executives, managers, and employees having a total personal commitment to the company's goal as a group. They are not only professional managers, clerks, engineers, technicians, machinists, and maintenance workers, but they are also "full-fledged family members." This Japanese organizational philosophy is *keiei-kazokushugi* or "management familism,"[5] and it has influenced Japan's unique recruitment practices and the nature of employer-employee relationships.

Recruitment of future employees is done with extreme care as if they are becoming immediate family members. Almost all Japanese companies administer a series of written examinations and interviews. These tests and interviews are designed to assess the candidates' general intelligence, motivation to work, personality, mental and physical health, and family background. Companies routinely commission background checks by an outside private investigation company *(kōshinjo)* that looks into every aspect of a candidate's private life. The most important personal qualifications for Japanese employers are excellent formal education, amicable personality, good family upbringing, and high motivation to work as a group member. Technical knowledge and previous work experience are secondary qualifications.

Japanese business organizations generally recruit their employees directly from schools once a year. Every October, employment examinations are given to those candidates who expect to graduate the following March. Large organizations neither make public announcement of employment examinations nor accept applications from schools indiscriminately. In most cases, personnel departments notify certain selected universities, colleges, and high schools of the availability of future positions. In addition, school officials in charge of placement, professors, teachers, and school principals contact those companies where their former graduates are already holding good positions. Well-established personal connections (called *kone* in Japanese) with these employers are extremely important in placing new graduates; nepotism and favoritism have never been considered undesirable in Japan as they are in the West. In fact, Japanese business organizations have a number of *gakubatsu* or "school cliques" based on *sempai-kohai kankei* (senior-junior relationships among alumni of the same universities). It is also common that two generations of workers come from the same families, because many Japanese children wish to work for the same company at which their fathers or uncles are employed. These particular personal relationships can be used effectively to promote group spirit and total dedication among the workers. It is true that different school cliques or family groups can become *habatsu* (factions within a company) because they tend to treat faction members much more favorably than nonfaction members. In some instances, *habatsu arasoni* (interfactional rivalries) can become vicious, but the feuding factions in the same company will unite against outsiders as rival siblings do when outsiders threaten the family.

Another important feature of Japanese business organizations is the unique employer-employee relationship. Japanese managers do not consider workers as "dispensable tools of production," but think of them as "family members" with great potential for creative and diligent work for many years. All major Japanese companies are still offering lifetime employment to new regular employees, and in turn, they expect the employees to devote their entire work lives to them. Because everyone enters at the bottom of the organizational hierarchy and works his way up to the top, even the president of a company was once just another new recruit. His salary is low compared to that of his American or European counterpart: the salary ratio between labor and top management in Japan is one to seven as compared to one to eighty in the United States.[6] In times of severe recession or business downturn, Japanese executives and senior managers are also willing to take a temporary pay cut before considering laying off their lower-ranking subordinates. This compassionate management attitude toward subordinates is the most important factor in making a Japanese business organization into a cohesive social institution.

Indoctrination and Training of New Employees

Prestowitz asserts that a typical Japanese company is more like the U.S. Marine Corps or an evangelical church than a company.[7] Indeed, indoctrination and training are carefully designed and executed for the sole purpose of making every employee a dedicated member of the company who will be willing to make a total commitment and to sacrifice toward achievement of collective corporate goals.

In Japan, indoctrination and training begin with an initiation training (shinyūshain kunren) and a ceremony on entering the company (nyūsha shiki). The initiation training begins with a one- or two-week camp at a mountain resort or a Buddhist temple site leased by the company. All new recruits are required to participate in physical, mental, and spiritual exercises designed to help them fully realize what their exact role will be when they begin working for the company. The purpose of this training camp is to build group spirit and to instill good work ethics and loyalty to the company. A typical training routine begins with a five-mile jog at dawn before breakfast, meditation, recitation of the company creed, and singing of the company song, followed by lectures of senior managers and prominent training consultants. The day ends at about

10:00 P.M. with an hour-long group discussion in which the new recruits reflect upon what they have learned that day. This group discussion is called *hansei kai* or "reflection meeting." Any individual participant or group that failed to live up to the expectation of the trainers must apologize and promise to do better the following day.

Throughout the day, the recruits break into small groups of five to seven and engage in various physical and mental activities. These activities always require intragroup cohesiveness and cooperation, as they are intentionally designed to promote group spirit and interdependence among all the participants. Praise and prizes are given to successful groups, but the members of unsuccessful groups are admonished and publicly humiliated during the training session.

For spiritual training, all trainees are required to participate in daily Zen meditation. They may have to meditate for a few hours in the unheated meditation hall of a Zen monastery on a cold early spring morning. Or they may be required to bathe in cold water under a waterfall. Japanese trainers seem to believe that mental toughness can be attained only through self-reflection and introspection under severe conditions. Group living in a dormitory and eating the same meals day after day also promote strong affinities and friendship among the group members who persevered the rigorous mental and physical training through cooperation and teamwork.

A similar method is also used for retraining middle managers. A caricature of this type of Japanese training was highlighted in a popular American movie, *Gung Ho*. Although this was just a Hollywood comedy, it portrays, somewhat accurately, what goes on in *jigoku no tokkun* or "training in hell."

Nyūsha shiki or "entering-the-company ceremony" is a uniquely Japanese way of inducting new employees. It is very much like an amalgam of the U.S. Marine Corps induction ceremony and an evangelical crusade. The president, top executives, senior workers, new recruits, and some of the recruits' parents attend the ceremony. It begins with singing of the company song and recitation of the company creed in unison. The master of ceremonies welcomes the parents, then presents the new recruits to the president and management. Next he calls on the president, who gives an impassioned lecture on the company's philosophy, mottos, social responsibility, and future goals, challenging every

35

new recruit to do his or her utmost to live up to these high ideals. The president also promises the parents that he will take responsibility for their children, educate and care for them. The master of ceremonies calls on the representative of the parents next. This representative first expresses the parents' gratitude and pleasure that their children are joining the company. He then says that the parents will support the company's business whenever possible and requests that the company discipline and guide their children. Then the master of ceremonies calls the roll of new members, reading each one's name and the school from which he or she has just graduated. Finally, he calls on the representative of the new recruits to make a response speech called *tōji* or "answer to the challenge." On behalf of his fellow-recruits, he expresses deep gratitude that they have been chosen to become new members of the company family and pledges total commitment and devotion to their work. At this ceremony, the company lapel pin is issued to every new recruit, and from then on, it must be worn proudly at all times. The ceremony ends with an elaborate banquet where all the participants celebrate this happy and memorable occasion.[8] The entire ceremony is intended to build a strong emotional identity with the company and a spirit of unity among all the participants.

Continuing the Spirit of Unity

This emotional identification with the company and the spirit of unity among the workers continue to be nurtured by *chōrei* or "morning pep-talk sessions," and by company-sponsored recreation trips, cultural classes, sports activities, and even matchmaking and marriage counseling.

Japanese factories and offices usually hold *chōrei* every morning before work begins. After gathering all of his subordinates, the manager in charge has them recite the company mottos and sing the company song together. He talks about the current business situation and challenges them to do their best that day.

Every Japanese company, regardless of its size, sponsors an annual company recreation trip (*ian ryokō*) for its managers and employees to a famous tourist destination in Japan or in a foreign country. Although employees can enjoy sightseeing, golf games, and fine food and drinks at company expense, the real purpose of the trip is to promote camaraderie and to strengthen emotional ties among all the participants. Top executives, senior managers, middle-level managers, and the rank and file travel together and participate in the company-sponsored dinner parties, sports activities, and sightseeing. The rank and file feel fortunate that they can meet and talk with their high-ranked superiors outside the formal confines of their offices. This trip is also intended to make the participants—most of whom couldn't afford such an expensive trip—feel obligated to the company.

Another popular way of nurturing close interpersonal relationships among the workers in Japan is to have a company-sponsored golf tournament and a banquet. The golfers play for the president's trophy and the prize money, and make friends among their fellow workers. Because golfing is very expensive in Japan, a golf tournament is a big treat for junior members of the company staff.

Japanese workers, especially male workers, frequently socialize among themselves after work. This socializing is called "*tsukiai*," and it is an extremely important means of establishing a network of personal friends among superiors, fellow-workers, and subordinates. Japanese managers and workers who do not participate in *tsukiai* are often stigmatized as aloof and unsociable, and they miss timely promotions and transfers.

Many large Japanese companies also sponsor free after-work classes such as English conversation, flower arrangement, cooking, tea ceremony, judo, kendo, and karate. On weekends, they sponsor such sports activities as tennis, softball, and baseball for the benefit of their employees. Larger multinational corporations hire several full-time English teachers and teach business English to their employees free of charge. Many of these companies also have a scholarship program for a few elite employees who want to study for a graduate degree in business administration, computer science, chemistry, electrical engineering, or the like at a prestigious foreign institution. Smaller companies provide financial subsidies to those who wish to take English classes at approved educational institutions.

Although a love marriage is considered ideal in today's Japan, many young Japanese find their marriage partners through an arranged marriage. One of the unofficial duties of a senior Japanese manager is matchmaking for his subordinates. He will constantly look for a prospective husband or wife for his subordinates and will volunteer to become an honorary go-between if he is asked to do so. *Shanai kekkon* or "marriage among fellow-work-ers" is therefore a very common occurrence. If the couple that he helped needs counseling about marital problems in the future, the manager may act as marriage counselor. There is no clear dichoto-my between work life and private life in Japan. The company not only supports the worker financially under an employment con-tract, but also provides strong emotional support and satisfies the social needs of every worker. Some companies even provide a wed-ding hall and open function rooms for an employee's wedding cer-emony and reception.

Compensation System and Employee Dependency

The Japanese system of paying compensation seems to have been designed to make employees dependent on the company they work for. One striking difference from the Western practice of wage payment is the concept of "living wage" or "need-based wage." An employee's economic needs are met by various allowances paid on top of the base pay—for example, family allowance, commuting allowance, and housing allowance; there is also a bonus system.[9] The family allowance is paid to a married worker to help him care for his dependents. Although the amount is nominal, a fixed amount is paid to him for his dependent-wife and for his children. The number of dependents entitled to receive the allowance is limited to an arbitrary number of three or four. Abegglen says that the family allowance is a dramatic example of a nonrational reward because the number of people in a worker's family has no connection to the economic goals of the company.[10] The commuting allowance can be seen as another nonrational pay-ment inasmuch as a worker who lives far away receives a higher allowance than his colleague who lives nearby. However, it provides an important incentive for long-term worker commitment as the average Japanese worker must spend two to four hours daily in commuting from his home in the suburb or a surrounding city. Such long-distance commuting is expensive. The commuting allowance is, therefore, consistent with the policy of lifetime employment because no employee should feel pressured to change his workplace when he changes his place of residence. Management also gives out monetary gifts on occasions of an employee's wedding, birth of a child, and death of a family member.

Japanese companies commonly pay a small starting salary and increase the pay gradually based on seniority and length of service. Because housing is extremely expensive in Japan, the housing allowance is the most important allowance for all Japanese workers. Typically, new employees are provided with housing at a nominal charge in a company dormitory. When they get married, they move into rent-free company housing or live, at the subsidized rent, in a condominium-apartment leased by the company. When they reach middle-management level and receive a higher salary, they are given a low-rate mortgage to buy a house in a suburb or a nearby city. These housing subsidies not only help the employees financially, but also provide them with psychological comfort and a strong sense of obligation toward the company.

The bonus system as practiced in Japan is another unique Japanese way of giving monetary compensation. Bonus payments are theoretically related to a company's output or profit during a given period. But in Japan, bonus payments have become almost as highly institutionalized as a regular wage since about 1950. Bonus payments are actually budgeted as overhead costs for the company. Every spring during *Shuntō* or "spring labor offensive," Japanese labor unions repeat negotiations with management on the amount of the bonus for their members. Japanese workers are given a bonus twice a year: at *Obon,* the midsummer Buddhist festival in July, and at *Kure,* the end of a calendar year in late December. Each bonus usually amounts to between two and a half months to three months of the base pay. Although the amount of bonus payment fluctuates a little from company to company, it is given to all workers regardless of the company's profit. Government workers, teachers and professors, policemen, firemen, and even workers in charitable organizations receive bonuses. In fact, the bonus payments are an essential part of Japanese workers' annual income and used for extra mortgage or car payments, vacation trips, customary gift purchases, and savings. The bonuses are more like "delayed payments of additional wages" paid in two separate installments. Abegglen says that the bonus system is essentially paternalistic in nature, that it is basically a gift of commendation from the management to the employees for the latter's contribution, not an obligation or duty.[11] In many companies, to make the employee feel personally obligated to the company and appreciative of the management's generosity, the president or the senior executive holds a ceremony and personally hands the bonus check to every employee. More recently, some companies have begun to use the bonus payment as an individual incentive, but they keep the amount of individual bonuses strictly confidential to prevent open conflict among the workers. Other companies intentionally pay bonuses as group incentives to encourage intergroup competition rather than individual competition.

Nenkō joretsu (promotion by seniority) and taishokukin seido (retirement fund system) are additional Japanese personnel management practices that cause employees to cling to their employer. Although promotion by seniority is often criticized as the reason for mediocrity among senior workers, the majority of Japanese companies reward workers of long tenure with higher wages or salaries to help them meet higher family expenses such as mortgage payments, tuition for children's education, recreational costs, and installment payments. Employees' retirement funds are kept by the company, not by a third party (life insurance or trust company), and the retirement funds are paid out in a lump sum at the time of retirement. Because this fund (commonly called ichijikin in Japan) can be very substantial for retirees with many years of service, all employees count heavily on this payment to pay off the mortgage balance or to save up as a nest egg. The lump-sum payment can be between five and ten times the retiree's annual base pay. This payment, however, can be in jeopardy if the company has a severe financial difficulty or goes bankrupt before the worker retires.

Nonregular Employees and Women Workers

Not all Japanese employees are regular employees (seishain) eligible for lifetime employment, automatic promotion based on length of service, and a large sum of retirement pay. Many are temporary hires (rinjishain) and part-time workers (pātotaimaa). They are hired only when they are needed to take on an extra work load and are laid off or fired whenever business slows down. Although many "temporary" workers are hired on a permanent basis, they cannot expect to be hired as regular employees. In many instances, these are women workers, who are not considered good prospects for permanent employment.

Japanese businesses have traditionally been a man's world. There are very few women in business except in clerical or secretarial jobs. And because Japanese society still maintains that a woman's primary role should be that of a full-time wife and mother, most Japanese employers expect women workers to take a temporary position and voluntarily resign when they get married or have their first child. Even today, an ideal and happy woman in Japan is seen as a "good wife and wise mother" *(ryōsai kenbo)*. This traditional ideology prevents Japanese female university graduates from taking on rewarding career opportunities.

Labor Union–Management Relationship

In December 1945, during the Allied Occupation, the Japanese Diet passed the Trade Union Law, which established a public policy similar to that of the United States. With instructions from General Douglas MacArthur, the Supreme Commander of the Allied Powers, the law was written using the Wagner Act as its model. However, the Japanese labor movement flourished for only a few years. In 1947, MacArthur banned a general strike, and in 1948, to control certain radical union activities, the law was revised to a more restrictive Taft-Hartley type. The heyday of organized labor was brought to an abrupt end in 1950 when the Korean War broke out. The so-called Red Purge was carried out on MacArthur's orders to get rid of Communist elements in Japanese labor unions.

The more significant reason why the Japanese labor movement patterned after the Western model failed is that it was culturally incompatible with the hierarchical Japanese society. According to Levine, "The concept of a mass movement, even one based upon conservative ideology, was foreign to the basic institutional relationships long characteristic of Japanese society. A horizontal amalgamation of workers ran counter to a tradition of vertical loyalties stemming from age-old consanguineal family system and feudal relationships."[12] Consequently, the Japanese labor movement took an entirely different direction, although the formal labor law was initially imported from the United States.

Japanese unions are *kigyō kumiai* or "enterprise unions" organized within individual enterprises and consisting only of the workers of that enterprise. For example, Toyota Motors' union membership consists of all of the Toyota workers. Machinists, electricians, sheet-metal workers, painters, clerical workers, and even lower supervisory staff belong to the same union. Negotiations with Toyota management over wage increases, bonus amounts, fringe benefits, and work rules are conducted by union representatives in the spirit of cooperation. In fact, the Toyota union works closely with management to beat Toyota's competitors in exchange for better wages and fringe benefits. Likewise, Nissan, Honda, Mazda, and Mitsubishi have their own similar enterprise unions.

Within the context of this enterprise union system, a strictly contractual and adversarial relationship between management and labor cannot be established. This Japanese style of management-labor relationship, called *nareai kankei* or "close emotional ties," is akin to a marital relationship. Because of this particular relationship, it is not uncommon that both union and management representatives know each other's positions and even reach general understanding on issues through off-the-record meetings before formal negotiation sessions.

Furthermore, it is important to point out that Japanese unions do not conduct their own independent training programs and certification of skills. Japanese enterprises prefer to conduct both classroom and on-the-job training using their own unique training methods. There are no standardized union classifications of skilled workers and clerical workers. In many instances, top union officials are on an "extended leave" from the enterprise and are allowed to return to their former positions whenever they finish union duties. This situation makes it almost impossible for these enterprise union members to move to another enterprise for a higher wage and better working conditions. The company, not the union, provides training, certification of skills, low-cost housing, low-mortgage financing, medical and dental care, retirement, and insurance plans. For these reasons, Japanese union members are far more loyal to their employer than their counterparts in Western countries.

chapter 3

Establishing Business Relations with the Japanese

The xenophobia of the Japanese people is well known throughout the world. Since they have lived and worked in a homogeneous society for many centuries, they are hesitant to accept foreigners and foreign ways. This unwillingness of the Japanese to
open up their country has invited strong criticism from the United
States and other trading partners. In particular, the Japanese are
accused of putting up nontariff barriers against foreign imports.
Nontariff barriers frequently pointed out by Americans are (1)
Japanese government policies and procedures designed to discrim-
inate against foreign imports, (2) the complex Japanese distribution
system, (3) the largely culture-based difficulty of acquiring existing
Japanese companies, (4) the difficulty of recruiting capable Japanese
employees to work for foreign firms, (5) the legal restrictions
imposed on U.S. lawyers who wish to practice in Japan, and (6) the
difficulty of doing business in the Japanese language.[1] Because
these "unfriendly" barriers have persisted, many American politicians and business leaders have angrily attacked Japan for not opening its consumer market to American products and meanwhile
accumulating a huge balance-of-trade surplus with the United
States. Marvin Wolf, a harsh Japan critic, accuses Japan of conspir-
ing against foreigners for its own self-interest. He says, "Japanese
business has come to be universally regarded with a near-mythic
mixture of fear and admiration, even envy. Demigods of trade, the
Japanese are seen as mysteriously energetic, tirelessly shrewd, part
of an irresistible tide. . . . The Japanese have brilliantly disguised
their conspiracy in a convincing cloak of free enterprises."[2] Other

Japanologists contend that some of these alleged barriers are culture-based misunderstandings and not a product of antiforeign conspiracy. Whether or not the Japanese conspiracy exists, American and other foreign companies have had difficulties in establishing equitable trade relations with Japanese companies.

Japanese managers and representatives who engage in international business speak fairly good English and appear to be Westernized, but they still conduct their business in a uniquely Japanese way. Because they are not as open and casual as Western businesspeople, Japanese businesspeople are difficult to approach without proper introduction. They are extremely cautious in choosing foreign business partners and hesitate to enter into business relations unless they are convinced of the prospective partners' credibility and reputation. The managers of large and prestigious Japanese companies are especially difficult to approach: they tend to be aloof, and they adhere to strict Japanese business protocol. Indeed, foreign businesspeople who hope to successfully conduct business transactions with the Japanese need to have a good understanding of proper Japanese ways of establishing and maintaining successful business relations.

Initiating Business Contacts

Making the initial contact with a Japanese company is not an easy task, because the proper Western approach can be improper and ineffective in the Japanese business context. For example, the most common American approaches such as writing a letter requesting an appointment, making a telephone call, and paying a visit in person are usually considered impolite and discourteous in Japan.

It is impossible to approach a prospective Japanese business associate by writing a letter of self-introduction and asking for an appointment. The letter will usually be ignored or put away in the pending file. A phone call from a stranger will be answered courteously, but it is unlikely that an appointment will be given. Except in rare instances, an introduction of one's own company or business by a letter or phone call has little effect. When writing a letter, the Japanese often start it with an apology, *Otegami de taihen shitsurei desu ga* or "I am sorry that I have to communicate with you by this letter, but . . ." They feel such a letter is too impersonal. If they have to introduce someone by a phone call, they will also apologize by saying, *Odenwa de shitsuri desu ga* or "I am sorry I have to talk to you over the phone, but . . ." because they still feel that a telephone call is an impolite means of initiating a business relationship. Even with today's easy access to highly advanced telecommunications technology, Japanese businesspeople rarely use telephone calls to initiate any new business. They usually avoid discussing any serious business matters with strangers unless they can first meet with them face to face. Japanese businesspeople with lower status will never call other businesspeople in higher-status positions for an initial appointment: that is a clear violation of business etiquette. In a few rare situations a letter of introduction or a phone call may work. For example, a personal letter from a senior professor to his former student for whom he found the present job will be honored. Or a phone call from the executive vice president of a large firm to the manager of its subsidiary company will be taken seriously. In these two cases, the implied message is "I am too busy to take my time and introduce this person face to face, but I demand that you honor my introduction anyway."

It is important to recognize that Japanese people usually do not flatly refuse to write a letter of introduction, as they are concerned about maintaining good interpersonal relations with their friends and acquaintances. However, they may contradict themselves and make negative comments informally over the telephone if they have any doubt about the person they are introducing. They are often compelled to take this seemingly dishonest action because they will be held responsible if something goes wrong later. It is also important to remember that obtaining a good introduction from a high-status person is not free in Japan. It is common practice for the person asking for an introduction to offer a monetary or nonmonetary gift to the introducer for this favor. The amount of money or the price of the gift is based on the recipient's social or professional status and on the size of the business transaction to be initiated.

A cold call is not only ineffective but also discourteous in initiating a business relationship in Japan. Almost all Japanese companies will politely refuse to grant an interview to an aggressive salesperson who comes in without an introduction or appointment. If the salesperson insists on meeting the manager in charge, a young assistant to the manager will come out and politely listen to what the visitor has to say, then end the conversation by saying that he will relay the message to his superior. Therefore, it is absolutely necessary for foreign businesspeople to learn culturally acceptable and effective ways of initiating business contacts in Japan.

Use of *Shōkaisha* (Introducer)

One of the best ways of initiating a viable business relationship in Japan is to obtain a letter of introduction *(shōkaijō)* from an introducer. A good introducer is a person respected and trusted by both parties involved. Not only is he expected to perform the task of matchmaking, but he is also expected to act as a mediator *(chūkaisha)* should a conflict arise in the future. He can be a personal friend, banker, company executive, officer of a chamber of commerce, director of a trade association, government official, high-level manager of an overseas subsidiary, or business consultant. A personal friend is the most reliable source of introduction because the Japanese prefer to do business with friends. And because every Japanese maintains a network of many close friends, he can easily find someone among his friends who can make a proper introduction. If he cannot find anyone, he can ask one of his friends to find a mutual friend of the prospective business associate. In this case, the introduction will be done in two stages. For example, Mr. Tanaka asks his friend, Mr. Suzuki, to introduce him to Mr. Ishii, who in turn introduces Mr. Tanaka to Mr. Yamamoto (the target of introduction), who is the mutual friend of Mr. Suzuki and Mr. Ishii. Among Japanese businesspeople, friendship can be more important than a mere business relationship. For this reason, they are initially much more interested in the personal backgrounds of future business partners such as their age, place of birth, formal education, and alumni connections than in their business backgrounds. They always want to establish common ground and a warm interpersonal relationship before they discuss business matters.

Like Japanese bureaucrats, Japanese bankers often act as intermediaries for their clients. They can be very useful as introducers, as they are usually trusted in Japanese society and have good connections in the business community. According to Japanese banking law, banks can own stocks in the companies to which they provide financing. It is a common practice for bank executives to go to work for client companies as managers of finance departments when they are about to reach minimum retirement age. They continue to act as liaison with their former employer and often act as go-betweens.

Japanese banks also routinely dispatch managers and supervisors whenever client companies need "special assistance" on financial matters such as restructuring loans and installing a new accounting system. In many instances when the client companies have serious financial problems due to mismanagement, Japanese banks dispatch their own managers and have them take over all the accounting functions of the troubled firms. This dispatching of bank employees is called *shikkō* or "on loan" because they are temporarily assigned to perform special assignments and are expected to return to their former positions in the banks. In some instances, a bank executive takes over the position of president and chief operating officer of a bankrupt company to protect his bank's loans and interests. Because of these close working relations, bankers are in a good position to provide an introduction and advice. In addition, large Japanese banks have an economic research department that generates important data and information on business activities of many Japanese corporations.

Business executives with large, reputable corporations can provide invaluable assistance in breaking the ice. The major function of Japanese executives is to expand and maintain personal connections among other executives for business purposes. They join prestigious golf clubs, civic clubs, hobby clubs, and study groups to meet new friends and socialize with them. A successful Japanese executive has extensive networks of many friends and associates in almost every sector of Japanese business circles.

In Japan, membership in chambers of commerce confers more prestige than in the United States. The membership is usually made up of presidents or vice presidents of small and medium-sized companies. Many top Japanese executives and politicians are former members of the Japan Junior Chamber of Commerce. The strong friendships developed during days of junior chamber activities seem to be carried on even after these executives become members of senior chambers of commerce. They get together for "alumni meetings" and trade favors with each other when they do business. Very successful junior chamber of commerce members

47

also join the Young Presidents Organization in order to expand their business connections. Foreign businesspeople who are active in chambers of commerce at home should take advantage of the strong ties among Japan's chambers of commerce members. A letter of introduction from the president of their local chapter will be very useful. American businesspeople should also consult the American Chamber of Commerce in Japan. The chamber has several publications that are helpful in understanding Japan and the Japanese from an American perspective.

Trade organizations in Japan are usually active in promoting their members' businesses. They frequently organize trade shows and seminars to exchange information on technology, marketing, and consumer trends. They also organize overseas study tours for their members to gain better understanding of international competition and to promote friendly relationships with foreign trade organizations. Staff members of these organizations are familiar with each member's business activities, and they can indicate which company might be a suitable business partner of a foreign company. For example, the Japan Electronics Manufacturers' Association could be a good place for an American electronic company to visit when it wishes to find a joint-venture partner in Japan. A letter of introduction from the president of the U.S. Electronic Manufacturers' Association to his Japanese counterpart can be a proper way to initiate a business relationship.

The American embassy in Tokyo has a business information center with a number of staff members who are assigned to assist American businesspeople wishing to do business in Japan. Many of the states have offices in Japan and are competing for direct investment and tourism into their own states. All of these offices have bilingual Japanese staff members who can assist American businesspeople in making contacts with Japanese companies. Since the Japanese have traditionally held their government officials in high regard, a letter of introduction from a proper foreign embassy official will be received very favorably. This is one quick way to establish credibility when starting a new business in Japan.

Today, a large number of Japanese companies have subsidiaries and branch offices all over the world. The most effective way of opening the door to successful business relations with a Japanese company is to contact the local branch manager, who can give an introduction to his home office. However, the first step is to win the trust and respect of that local branch manager by getting to know him personally. He will never make any introduction unless he is convinced that he and his company will benefit from it. He will certainly be cautious about recommending anyone because he must take full responsibility if something goes wrong. Aggressive American business executives are often tempted to bypass the local branch manager and go directly to the president or vice president at the head office. This is a big mistake. The local manager can actually destroy any prospect of establishing a business relationship if he feels that he has been bypassed or overlooked. Japanese top executives usually do not make decisions on their own. They rely heavily on the judgment of their local managers whenever they consider establishing a new business relationship with a foreign company. It is, therefore, crucial to make friends and allies among the Japanese managers who are stationed overseas and representing their parent companies.

49

Reputable international business consultants can be helpful in establishing new business relations with Japanese companies. Several American consulting companies and American accounting firms provide consulting services. Large Japanese banks usually provide similar services to their client companies. Selecting a consulting company is not an easy task, because not all consulting companies are considered trustworthy and proficient. The reputation of an individual consultant and his affiliation should be carefully checked before a contract is signed. A consultant should be a business and/or technical expert rather than an English-language expert. Generally speaking, American businesspeople are prone to hire speakers of good English who may or may not have professional and technical knowledge and sufficient experience. Or they may hire American-educated Japanese females with whom Japanese businessmen will hesitate to do business because they are generally considered too "Americanized and incompetent." Some American-educated Japanese consultants have a condescending attitude toward the Japanese way of doing business and will not be effective at all. An international business consultant should be bilingual and bicultural, but at the same time, he or she must have substantial expertise and many years of experience in the particular segment of business for which he or she is asked to consult.

The First Contact with Japanese Businesspeople

Generally speaking, Westerners are more aggressive and self-reliant than their Japanese counterparts, and they prefer to cultivate their own business contacts without involving others. They might think that a letter of introduction or a phone call from a mutual friend to the prospective Japanese business partner will be sufficient to open the door for a new business relationship. However, their tactic will not work well in Japan. The most effective way to initiate a business contact is to have the introducer arrange a face-to-face meeting with a Japanese businessman solely for the purpose of *aisatsu* or "formal introduction." The initial meeting can take place either at the Japanese businessman's office or at a restaurant. On the office visit, the introducer will introduce the American businessman to the Japanese manager in charge of the international division, young staff members, and one or two top executives. Although he will introduce the American formally at this time, he would have informed the Japanese side of the foreign visitor's company and his personal profile before this first visit.

Exchanging *Meishi* or Business Cards

Every introduction starts with exchanging of *meishi* (business cards); the exchange serves a number of useful and important functions. The business card not only provides the person's name, but also his job title, company name, address, telephone number, facsimile number, and e-mail address. In Japan, the job title, company affiliation and seniority in rank or age actually dictate how language is used, the manner of speaking, and nonverbal behavior. In other words, exchanging of *meishi* instantaneously clarifies the proper status relationship between individuals meeting for the first time. Every foreign businessperson should follow the Japanese custom of exchanging *meishi*: (1) He should have his business card printed in both English and Japanese on high-quality paper and have a sufficient number of cards. (2) He should have them handy at all times so that he can hand one out immediately upon meeting new Japanese business associates.★ (3) He should not pass out his *meishi* like passing out playing cards at a card table. (4) If he is already sitting down, he should stand up and hand the cards out to every person with a slight bow as if it were an expensive and fragile gift. (5) He should extend his card out with the Japanese side up, facing the recipient so that it can be read easily. (6) He should receive the other person's business card with both hands with a slight bow and should scan it immediately for vital information. (7) He should try to use the name of his Japanese counterpart in the course of conversation and learn to pronounce it correctly. (8) When he is accompanying his superior, he should hand out his *meishi* only after he has been introduced. When exchanging business cards, it is customary to say the person's last name and then say "*Hajime mashite dōzo yoroshiku*," more or less equivalent to "How do you do! It's nice to meet you" in English. In this situation, the most important thing to remember is to exchange cards in hierarchical order. For example, the American visitor must exchange business cards with the highest-ranked Japanese executive first, then with the second-highest-ranked manager, next with the lower-ranked managers. Westerners often make the mistake of exchanging the card first with the Japanese person who happens to be standing closest. They should take time and observe how the Japanese who are present show deference to each other. One of them usually signals to the visitor nonverbally (with a hand gesture or body motion) whom he should greet first and exchange business cards with. In some instances, a young Japanese assistant hesitates or avoids exchanging his business card with a high-ranking foreign visitor in front of the executives of his company. He knows that he does not deserve to be recognized as an equal in this situation. Especially when the executives from a foreign company meet with the executives of his company, he will intentionally step aside and have the top executives from both sides

★ Many American businessmen keep business cards in their wallets in their back pockets. They should not keep *meishi* in the wallet because cards can become warped, soiled, and even smelly. They should buy a nice *meishi ire* or "small wallet" to keep their business cards in. It should be noted that *meishi ire* made by Dunhill, Guchi, Louis Vuitton or Christian Dior are status symbols among Japanese businessmen.

greet each other first. It may seem strange to foreign executives that a young Japanese staff member who acts as interpreter does not volunteer to give his *meishi* in front of his senior managers, but this is the proper etiquette for a young and lower-ranked Japanese businessman. However, it is acceptable for him to give out his card after his superior gives him permission to do so. If he is asked for it by a foreign executive, he usually says that he will give it to him after the formal meeting and in private.★

Japanese Names and Pronunciation

Even though Japanese businesspeople's names are romanized and printed on their *meishi*, foreign businesspeople may find them difficult to pronounce correctly unless they have studied Japanese. Except for five vowels [a], [e], [i], [o], [u] and a consonant [n], Japanese alphabet letters are usually romanized with two or three English characters. Many Americans make the mistake of bunching Japanese syllables together and pronouncing them with strong English accents. For example, *Nakasone*, the name of Japan's former prime minister, should be pronounced as *na-ka-so-ne*, not "nakasone." *Aoki* is the name of a famous Japanese golfer, and his name is often mispronounced as "A-oki." It should be pronounced as [a] in father, [o] in horse and *ki* or *a-o-ki*. Or *Kato*, a common Japanese name, should be pronounced as *ka-tō*, not "kay-tow." One important piece of advice to Westerners is that they should refrain from giving new Japanese business associates English nicknames simply because their Japanese names are difficult to pronounce. It is better to ask them how to pronounce their names correctly than to insult them by mispronouncing those names.†

★ It is acceptable not to offer a business card to a young Japanese assistant. He will be embarrassed if he is forced to exchange *meishi* in front of top executives of his company.

† When a Japanese businessman cannot read the name on *meishi*, he might ask nonchalantly, "Your name is very unusual, isn't it?" by which he means, "I do not know how to pronounce your name. Please tell me again!"

Hierarchy of Seating

The Japanese protocols of seating are frequently puzzling for uninformed American businesspeople. Participants in a business meeting in Japan are seated in the exact order of their relative ranking. Americans often make the mistake of seating themselves without being invited to sit down or taking a seat nonchalantly without paying close attention to status differences. For example, the vice president of an American company and his assistant are visiting the president of a Japanese company for the first time. The American visitors will be met by young staff members of the president's office *(shachō shitsu)* who speak English and be escorted to the executive meeting room. They will be asked to sit in specific chairs for honored guests, usually on far ends of the room against the wall and away from the door, and wait for the president to come in. The interpreter usually sits on a stool between the American vice president and the Japanese president.

It is an unforgivable violation of the protocol to switch seats just for one's own convenience. Each seat represents a different degree of respect paid to the person who occupies it. Each Japanese executive or staff member knows his rank relative to other Japanese participants, and he gives up his seat to a higher-ranked person coming in later and moves down to a lower seat. Foreign visitors need to closely observe the unwritten rules of proper seating by following the verbal or nonverbal cues given by the Japanese host and to pay attention to who sits where on the Japanese side.

Socializing for Business Contacts

Another effective way of initiating a business contact is to socialize first over a nice lunch or dinner. Westerners usually have a business lunch, but Japanese businessmen prefer to have a "social dinner." The Japanese have two specific reasons for this preference: (1) They prefer to socialize with the prospective business partners and get to know them personally before they conduct any serious business discussions. (2) Since the Japanese workday starts at 9:00 A.M. or

9:30 A.M. and ends at 5:30 P.M. or 6:00 P.M., they have a much shorter work period before lunch time.*

Under the usual circumstance, the introducer will make the dinner arrangement and invite the other party. He briefly explains to the other party the purpose of getting together for dinner, but he does not give any specific information regarding business matters. He might simply say, "Mr. Kato, my good friend, Mr. Smith, wants to meet with you. He is the president of Innovation and Technology Company in California. Several years ago, he and I attended the Top Executive Seminar at the Harvard Business School in Boston. Now he is interested in doing business with a reputable Japanese company. I suggested that he should get together with you first before he talks to any other company. Can you meet with him on next Tuesday?" If Mr. Kato hesitates to accept the invitation, the introducer would assure him that he will not be expected to make any commitment and that this will be just a "get-acquainted dinner" to introduce Mr. Smith.

When Mr. Kato agrees to meet with Mr. Smith, the latter will make the arrangements for this first dinner meeting (although the introducer can advise what to do). The choice of a restaurant is very important, as it reflects Mr. Smith's integrity and his attitude toward Mr. Kato. The restaurant should be a reputable establishment with good ambience; tasty, high-quality food; and excellent personal service; it should also provide privacy. Since this dinner meeting is to be used only for socializing, substantive business matters will not be discussed.

At the beginning of the dinner, everyone exchanges *meishi* and engages in small talk. They also ask personal questions. Westerners might consider some of the questions that the Japanese ask of new business associates too personal. They may feel uneasy or even offended by these questions that pry into personal matters not related to professional qualifications and business acumen, but this is a socially acceptable way in Japan for potential business partners to assess each other's personality and backgrounds. The

---

* Japanese businessmen spend at least an hour and a half commuting each way, so they cannot come to work early. This is the major reason why they almost never hold breakfast meetings. They may have to stay at a nearby hotel to make the early breakfast meeting scheduled for a foreign business associate's convenience.

answers to these questions provide the Japanese with information that will help them anticipate the other side's attitude, willingness to cooperate, and possible reactions on future business dealings. In short, they want to establish rapport and interpersonal trust by getting to know everyone personally. They do not hesitate to invest lots of time and money to attain this first objective when starting a new business relationship. The Japanese have a strong aversion to surprises.

The most commonly asked questions are as follows:

"What university did you graduate from?"

"Where were you born?"

"What year were you born?"

"Do you play golf? What is your handicap?"

"How many times have you visited Japan?"

"Do you speak Japanese?"

"Do you like Japanese food?"

"How long have you been working for this company?"

"What is your relationship with your introducer?"

"What is your blood type, if I may ask?"

The answer to each of the above questions has culturally important implications in Japan when judging each individual's personal worth. Graduation from one of the more prestigious universities is a good indication that the person is intelligent and comes from a good family. Getting into a good university in Japan is a family affair. Parents must have enough money to hire a private tutor for the child or to send him to a private preparatory school.

The place of birth is a factor of common ground. People born in the same city or prefecture feel a strong sense of affinity. Place of birth also indicates whether the individual is a sophisticated city person or a country bumpkin.

Age is an important factor in Japanese society. Seniority in age means that a person has extensive practical knowledge, many years of experience, wisdom, good business contacts, and usually a higher status. Some Japanese still believe in the Chinese horoscopes or the twelve signs named after twelve different animals (rat, ox, tiger, rabbit, dragon, snake, horse, goat, monkey, rooster, dog, and pig) and use them in judging another person's personality. Each year is named after one of the animals, and it is believed that people born during that year inherit some of the personality characteristics of that animal. Compatibility between certain animal signs is considered important for personal relationships such as marriages and joint-ventures.

Having a low golf handicap and owning a membership in a famous country club indicates that the individual is rich and has a good network of high-level businessman friends.

Having been to Japan many times, liking Japanese foods, and speaking Japanese show that the person likes and respects Japan and the Japanese.

Japanese businesspeople always ask about the years of service with a company, because long tenure with one company means loyalty, dedication, trust, stability, power, and influence. A person who moves from one company to another—even for promotion—is often called a "migratory bird" and considered to be an opportunist who cannot be trusted. American executives proud of their career advancement through switching jobs should not volunteer to talk about frequent job-hopping even for better positions.★

Many Japanese also believe in the relationship between blood type and personality. The person with type O blood is considered to be generous, bold, pleasant, and optimistic. The person with type A blood is meticulous, hardworking, intelligent, but rather timid. The person with type B blood is nervous, pessimistic, cunning, thrifty, and suspicious. The person with type AB blood vacillates between A- and B-type behaviors.

Japanese businesspeople want to know all of this personal information to help them predict the reactions of new business partners. However, compatibility based on Chinese horoscopes and

---

★ When an American businessman who has been with the company for a few years is asked of his tenure, he will answer honestly, "Oh, I've been with this company for a couple of years." This is a bad answer! He should say, "Oh, I've been with this company for three years, but I have been in the industry for more than fifteen years."

personality based on blood types is not taken as seriously as other personal information. In fact, many younger Japanese think that these are mere superstitions.

Quite often, American executives unknowingly violate social taboos in the initial business meeting or socializing situations. The most common mistakes are the following: (1) They tend to "blow their own horn" too loud and brag about their personal accomplishments. (2) They become too friendly too fast and want to use a person's first name right away. (3) They are quick to tell jokes that cannot be understood. (4) They often praise their wives in public and even talk freely about their divorces, remarriages, former wives, and stepchildren. These topics are not socially acceptable in Japan. Japanese businessmen will talk about their children, but very little about their wives. They will not talk at all about a divorce or any girlfriends.

The answer to the question regarding the relationship with the introducer is the most crucial one; it will determine how seriously the introduction should be taken. If the relationship is a short and casual one, the introduction is meaningless. In other words, it must have been a solid and long-term relationship to make the introduction viable.

Golf as an Icebreaker

Playing a round of golf with prospective Japanese business associates is an excellent icebreaker. It is one of the popular ways to get acquainted with new friends informally. Japanese business executives often introduce each other on a golf course. Since they spend between four and six hours together, they have ample time to talk about themselves and to informally discuss a few business-related matters. They also try to see how other golf partners react to various situations, and carefully assess everyone's personality, temperament, and compatibility. For example, a golfer who swears out loud when he misses a shot or cheats on keeping his score would naturally be considered a bad risk as a business partner. On the other hand, a golfer who does not show his temper and is cheerful under pressure is considered to have the makings of a good business partner. It is very important not to embarrass Japanese partners by beating them too soundly; naked competitiveness will not be appreciated. In some instances, good Japanese golfers intentionally lose some holes so that they do not shame poor golfing partners. Good manners on a golf course will win many friends among Japanese business associates.

When they finish the game, the players will all get together on the "nineteenth hole" or cocktail lounge and continue to socialize with each other. If they have been able to establish good rapport and friendship, they will promise to meet again for another round of golf or for a preliminary business discussion at their offices.

Personality and Status of Initial Team Members

The most important consideration in initiating business contacts in Japan is to select people who are capable of establishing good rapport and mutual trust with the Japanese side. On the first visit, it is customary in Japan to send a team of at least three people—one senior executive, one middle manager, and one young junior assistant. The senior executive plays a ceremonial role of rendering credibility, the middle manager takes on the task of conducting business discussions, and the young assistant acts as interpreter and coordinator. This team approach is a stark contrast to the one-man team of the American senior executive who represents his company single-handedly. Since the first impression has a strong influence on subsequent interpersonal interactions, foreign businesspeople must present the best possible "face" of the company they represent and act properly according to Japanese business protocol.

Personality and Attitude of Foreign Businesspeople

Most American companies choose "proud professional sales executives"[3] to initiate business contacts with Japanese companies. These kinds of Americans, however, cannot accomplish their mission successfully because they fail to realize the cultural differences in common practices of selling and buying between Japan and the United States. One important difference between Japanese and Western concepts of selling is that in Japan, sales are being made through good interpersonal relations with customers, not through persuasion based on facts and figures only. Another important difference is that the buyer is always regarded as having superior status to the salesperson, regardless of the circumstances. Rugged individualism is also frowned upon as egotistical, and the team effort, not that of a certain individual, is very important. In a nutshell, amicable and patient managers with good human relations skills should be dispatched to Japan, and they should go about establishing long-term business relationships with their Japanese counterparts. American companies should avoid sending managers with old stereotype images of Japan and the Japanese. It is still true that some American executives have strong ethnocentrism and a desire to downgrade the significant achievements made by Japan in high-tech industries, international business, and finance over the past few decades. This arrogant attitude becomes a serious hindrance to establishing good rapport and mutual respect. In Japan, the salesperson is always expected to assume a low posture of humility regardless of his professional status. For example, a senior vice president of a large Japanese company bows politely and uses respect language to a younger department head of another company if he is there to sell his company's products.

Matching of Status with Japanese Counterparts

The status of the foreign company representative should match that of the Japanese counterpart. As in the case of international diplomatic protocol, it is extremely rude to send a lower-ranking foreign company official to meet a high-ranking executive of the Japanese company. The initial greeting should be conducted properly by the highest-ranking executive, if it is at all possible. Ideally, the president of the foreign company should pay a courtesy visit *(hyōkei hōmon)* to the president of the Japanese company. If the foreign company president is not available, the executive vice president should represent the president. In this case, the executive vice president should clearly say that he is representing the president, who could not come for a good reason. For example, he should say, "President Smith regrets that he could not come on this trip, but he sends his regards to you. He needs to attend an important executive meeting on a new project. I will convey your message to him when I return to the home office." He should never say, "I am the official representative, and I am authorized to talk with you regarding our new business relationship," even if he is indeed in charge of new business in Japan. As mentioned earlier, it is always wise to send a small team of representatives of different ranks and specializations. The team may consist of an executive vice president, a senior manager (equivalent to a Japanese department head), and an assistant manager. The senior manager and his assistant may engage in some specific business discussion with their Japanese counterparts on the first visit, but the executive vice president should play only a ceremonial role. In some instances, the executive vice president may be asked to socialize with the Japanese executives of equal rank on a golf course while his subordinates are engaging in preliminary business discussions.

Effectiveness of Female Executives

With the stronger enforcement of the Equal Employment Opportunities Act and affirmative action legislation by the United States government, many professionally capable women now occupy top executive positions in American corporations. The question arises whether an American female executive can establish and maintain a viable business relationship with her Japanese male counterpart. A simple answer is that in the traditionally male-dominated Japanese business community, female executives do not fare well except in very rare circumstances. One serious drawback for American female executives is that they are usually excluded from late evening outings at hostess bars and nightclubs where *honne* or true feeling on business matters is revealed. Their Japanese counterparts worry that American female executives will feel uncomfortable and out of place at these establishments. They still prefer to talk about serious business off and on between small talk, drinking and eating, singing karaoke songs, and flirting with young hostesses.[4]

If an American female executive wishes to be effective, she should dress conservatively and act professionally in all of her encounters with Japanese males. She should make special efforts to make clear that she is a businesswoman, not a female who enjoys men's admiration. It is a good idea to have an older American manager accompany her as "senior advisor" and to ask him to take on socializing duties reserved for men only. It is also advisable to give him a "big title" that gives him credibility in the eyes of the Japanese, even if such a title does not exist at the home office.

Gift Giving at the First Meeting

It is customary in Japan that new business relations begin with gift exchanges. The value and the type of gifts depend on the size of future businesses and the status of the relationship. For example, the executive vice president of an American computer chip manufacturer may bring a case of expensive California wine as a gift for the president of the Japanese company to whom he intends to sell the computer chips. In exchange, the Japanese president presents an expensive Italian silk necktie and a box of golf balls with his company logo. Most Japanese companies have several gift items such as neckties, mini calculators, alarm clocks, electronic address books and business calendars, or pearl earrings or brooches that are used for gift exchanges.

There are two kinds of gifts: a small gift exchanged as a token of friendship and an expensive gift often called "a gift with an ulterior motive." The latter is obviously intended to create a sense of obligation on the part of the recipient, who will be obligated to make an extra effort to accommodate the wishes of the giver. If he would like to cancel this obligation, he can return a gift of similar value immediately. Whichever kind of gift it may be, international businesspeople should not forget to bring an appropriate gift when they initiate business contacts with the Japanese. One last piece of advice to Westerners is that they must not say how expensive the gift item is because it is social etiquette in Japan to verbally downgrade the value of the gift. The Japanese typically say, "This is a small token of our appreciation" or "Such a humble gift like this may not suit your taste, but . . . ," even if everyone knows that it is an expensive one. And they expect the recipient to deny that statement by saying, "Oh, you should not have given us such an expensive gift. We really do not deserve it!" This is merely a social ritual that every Japanese is expected to engage in. Therefore, it is a good idea even for foreign businesspeople to follow this social custom and be modest when they are presenting gifts to their Japanese counterparts.

Interpersonal Communication and Sales Presentation

I nterpersonal communication has become the most important means of communication in today's international business. Thanks to the tremendous technological advancements in the electronic communications media and in air transportation, international businessmen are able to conduct their businesses via worldwide networks of fiber-optic links for long-distance telephones, facsimile machines, Internet computer networks, and video-conferencing systems. They routinely send and receive both verbal and nonverbal messages instantaneously through these means of communication. They frequently fly to and from foreign countries to hold meetings with their business associates overseas. In fact, millions of international businesspeople crisscross the Pacific and Atlantic oceans every day to hold face-to-face meetings. However, they still encounter many problems in communicating with each other, as they usually do not share the same linguistic and cultural backgrounds. Misunderstandings often occur because one or both sides do not have adequate language skills and because they, knowingly or unknowingly, violate each other's cultural norms or expectations.

Interpersonal Communication

In communicating with the Japanese, foreign businesspeople need to recognize several important variables that directly affect the process and the outcome of interpersonal communication. These variables are communication skills, attitudes, level of technical knowledge, cultural factors, purpose of communication, and communication context.

Communication Skills

Communication skills can be categorized into speaking, listening, reading, writing, and thinking or reasoning. Ideally, both parties engaging in interpersonal communication have the same or similar level of competency in these communication skills. In intercultural communication, however, it is virtually impossible to expect that two parties have the same proficiency in the language of communication. In most instances, one party is forced to speak in a foreign language while the other party speaks his or her own native language. For example, in Japanese–American business communication settings, the Japanese are almost always compelled to speak in English because very few Americans can speak good Japanese. Consequently, the Japanese are severely handicapped unless they have lived and worked among Americans for many years. The majority of the Japanese who speak English have a rather limited vocabulary and a thick Japanese accent. They may have difficulty in pronouncing certain English sounds. They may also have difficulty in understanding what the American businesspeople are trying to communicate in English at their normal rate of speech. Many Japanese businessmen who speak "passable conversational English" do not understand English idioms and technical jargon. Unless they are really bilingual, they must think first in Japanese and then translate that thought into English. They must go through the same process in the reverse order when they hear English. Naturally, this mental process of translating and retranslating requires much more time for them.

When Americans encounter this situation, they have a strong tendency to dominate verbal interactions by talking incessantly. They become impatient and even volunteer to complete unfinished sentences when the Japanese seem to be struggling with their English. They may even think that the Japanese are incompetent. This is not the proper way to carry on effective interpersonal communication. American businesspeople should learn to be more patient with nonnative speakers of English, refrain from dominating verbal interactions with them, and avoid making a hasty and erroneous judgment of their professional qualifications based only on their English-language competency.

Attitudes

Having positive attitudes is important for native speakers of English when communicating with foreigners who do not speak good English. Some nonnative speakers of English, particularly Japanese people, suffer from an inferiority complex because of their inadequate English-language facility. Many Japanese businesspeople become apologetic and tentative when they speak English. They may even display peculiar and annoying verbal habits. These habits might be repeating of "You know, you know," "I don't know, but . . . ," or "And uh . . ." before or after each statement. And they might frequently interject "I'm sorry" whenever they make a mistake in pronouncing difficult English words. They may also shift their eyes and look away when they should be making good eye contact. Some of them smile nervously and even show jittery body movements when they get excited.

Such poor communication behavior can be grossly misunderstood by the average American who has never had to communicate in a foreign language. In the United States, people are sometimes categorized in different social classes by the type of English they speak. It is generally assumed that "standard American English" is spoken by the rich and the educated, "colloquial American English" by lower-middle-class workers and laborers, and "substandard American English" with foreign accents by the uneducated and by new immigrants. Nist labeled these types of English as "American social class-lects" with differing social acceptance and prestige. He classifies them as "Acrolect," "Mesilect," and "Basilect."[1] It is unfortunate, but the kind of broken English spoken by the Japanese, satirically called "Japlish," can be categorized as "substandard English." Despite the fact that many Japanese businesspeople may speak funny English, American businesspeople should appreciate their effort in trying to communicate in English.

English is not their native language. Undoubtedly, having positive attitudes will facilitate better outcomes of interpersonal communication with the Japanese.

Level of Technical Knowledge

Accurate assessment of the knowledge level of the other party is an important prerequisite for successful interpersonal communication. In intercultural communication, it is ideal that both parties have the same level of technical or professional knowledge in both languages about the subject under discussion. This ideal is practically never realized. The Japanese might have good knowledge of it in Japanese, but they may not know all of the technical terminology and idiomatic expressions in English. In this case, the subject must be explained in nontechnical language or reference must be made to written materials more frequently. On the other hand, it is possible for a Japanese engineer and a foreign engineer to overcome each other's language inadequacies if they have common interests and a similar level of technical knowledge.

Cultural Factors

In all interpersonal communication situations in Japan, social role relationships among individual participants are critical. Japanese people act and react in certain ways expected of them according to their respective social positions. They tend to be formal and reserved, and they are always conscious of their status in relation to that of others. In contrast, Westerners are usually informal, friendly, and humorous in their interpersonal interactions. They often unknowingly violate the rather complicated Japanese social etiquette. The most important Japanese cultural factor is to recognize the so-called status game that is always played out in interpersonal communication situations. The Japanese routinely engage in dichotomous behaviors—the respectful and polite behavior toward a person of superior status, and the condescending and even rude behavior toward a person of inferior status. The Japanese call each other by their titles and use an appropriate level of politeness when speaking to superiors. For example, Mr. Sato, a section chief *(kachō)* calls Mr. Tanaka, his department head *(buchō)* by using the latter's title—Tanaka *buchō* (Department Head Tanaka)—but Mr. Tanaka calls Mr. Sato by saying *kachō* (Section Chief) or Sato-*kun*.★ At a Japanese office, it is impolite even for a senior manager to call his subordinate by his last name only. He rarely uses the subordinate's first name unless he is scolding him for a big mistake. For this reason, almost all Japanese businesspeople will feel uncomfortable if their new Western business associates call them by their first name or nickname. At the same time, they feel uneasy calling their Western counterparts by their first name, even if they are invited to do so.

The Japanese language also has a rich and elaborate vocabulary of status-indicative expressions. For example, there are several different pronouns referring to "you" and "I," and different verb forms used in specific situations. Although choice of polite expressions may not be so important when speaking in English, Japanese businesspeople still feel uncomfortable if status differences are totally ignored. Indeed, it is important to recognize the status-consciousness of the Japanese at all times by speaking to them politely.

The second cultural factor is excessive concern of the Japanese over maintaining smooth and pleasant social relationships; this concern makes them respond in indirect and vague ways. They often use prolonged silence when they are unsure of what to say. Sometimes, if a question is difficult or embarrassing to answer, they even pretend that they did not hear it.

The Japanese tend to display two different faces—*sotozura* (face toward outsiders) and *uchizura* (face toward insiders). Just to be polite, they may smile and nod frequently to show a "happy and pleasant face" to outsiders. They may also say "yes" if they feel pressured to do so when, in fact, they do not mean "yes." This answer is called a *kara henji* or "empty answer." They also nod frequently when they are listening, and this nodding is called *aizuchi* or "agreeing signal." Japanese businesspeople may use these convenient social responses when they are forced to listen to unreasonable demands from persons of higher status. They never try to con-

★ *Kun* is a suffix used after the surname of a person of lower status by a superior. *Sama* or *san* is used for a person of superior status by an inferior.

front and reason with them as most Americans would do in such situations. In glaring contrast, however, this smiling face of the same Japanese can turn into a stern and fierce-looking one. Japanese men use impolite language and gestures when they scold "social inferiors" such as their subordinates, salesclerks, and servants. For example, an irate Japanese manager might show *uchizura* and scold his subordinate by shouting loudly and by pointing at him with his index finger. American subordinates working under a Japanese manager will find these two different faces disturbing and confusing, to say the least.

The third cultural factor is differences in role expectations. Culture assigns specific roles to every member of a society, and cultural differences in role expectations cause difficulties in interpersonal intercultural communication. For example, a Japanese senior executive and an American senior executive play different roles. At work, the Japanese executive is expected to play the role of a mild-mannered gentleman who acts as mediator or facilitator of decisions. He spends most of the workday meeting with his colleagues and subordinates and entertaining important clients. If he is asked, he helps his subordinates with private matters such as arranging marriages, finding jobs, recommending good schools, counseling on family problems, and so on. At home, the Japanese executive almost never performs any house chores for his wife. He will never go to a supermarket with his wife because he never wants to be seen by his acquaintances pushing around a shopping cart. He has his wife take full charge of family finances and the children's education.

In contrast, the American executive is a tough, self-reliant, and confident individual who aggressively takes on diverse tasks and makes decisions on his own. At the same time, he is friendly, good-humored, and straightforward in his dealings with both superiors and inferiors. He also volunteers to help his wife and children whenever he can find time to do so. These differences in role expectations can cause communication difficulties. For example, a visiting Japanese executive wants his American counterpart to go out socializing after work. But the American executive flatly declines, saying, "I have to go home because my wife is cooking a nice dinner for me tonight." The Japanese executive finds such an answer unfathomable. In this situation, he would never have to go home to his wife but would, instead, socialize with his business associate.

The fourth cultural factor is concealment of emotions. It is not that the Japanese do not have emotions, but they tend to conceal their emotions in formal face-to-face encounters with strangers and are not generous with compliments. Westerners who do not understand this Japanese cultural trait find the Japanese to be unfeeling, poker-faced, and even cold.

Purpose of Communication

In all interpersonal encounters, the purpose of communication inevitably controls both the verbal and the nonverbal behavior of the participants. In intercultural communication, however, the same purpose of communication may not produce the same communication behavior. In the Japanese business context, the content of the face-to-face communication often does not indicate its purpose. Japanese businessmen are not as purpose-oriented and logical as their American counterparts; they are more concerned about smooth interpersonal relations than about efficient communication. The Japanese spend much more time in small talk, and they interrupt business discussions with frequent tea or coffee breaks. They may change the subject of discussion abruptly when they feel that social tension has been created among the participants. They will not adhere to the purpose of communication closely if they feel it will create an uneasy atmosphere of disagreement or confrontation. Nevertheless, the Japanese do not favor humorous statements or jokes in a serious business meeting. Westerners should refrain from giving unrestrained praise and compliments and from using emotional appeals, strong voices, or animated big gestures because such behavior will undoubtedly embarrass and even offend the Japanese.

Communication Context

In intercultural interpersonal communication, recognizing the context of communication can be extremely important. For example, an American businessman conducting a business meeting in Tokyo is expected to conform to the Japanese style of communication, while a Japanese businessman in New York is expected to go along with the American style. Disregard of either of these communication contexts can cause serious communication difficulties. The American businessman doing business in Tokyo is expected to engage in certain verbal and nonverbal rituals peculiar to Japanese communication settings. He must exchange greetings and business cards with several of his new Japanese business associates. He must shake hands and bow, smiling politely. He must even "apologize" for his intrusion, especially when he is meeting with a senior Japanese executive. Because gift giving is an institutionalized custom of Japan in establishing and maintaining business relationships, he is expected to present a proper gift on his first visit. He may have to engage in small talk for a longer time than he is accustomed to before he is invited to talk about business matters. In addition, he will have to pay close attention to where he sits and to when, to whom, and how much he can talk. One striking difference between Japanese and American ways of doing business is that Japanese businessmen prefer to meet informally in restaurants and hostess bars and on golf courses. They often engage in business discussions intermittently while eating, drinking, and playing golf. They wish to avoid the formal contexts of a conference room especially when they need to discuss sensitive issues.

Likewise, the Japanese businessman working in New York must adapt to the American style of communication. He must know that he will meet only those American business associates who are directly involved in the business at hand. He can neither impress them with an expensive gift, nor expect to be invited to high-class restaurants, hostess bars, and golf courses for business discussions. Consequently, he must behave in a more businesslike manner and must present his ideas clearly from the very beginning during his formal office visit. He will be extremely disappointed if he expects to have "after-hour socials" to float his ideas around and obtain reactions informally. He need not bring any expensive gift with him because most American businessmen will interpret it as a form of a bribe. In other words, he must distinguish business and social contexts of communication when he is doing business in the United States.

Means of Communication

Despite the advancement of electronic means of communication such as international telephones, facsimiles, and computer networks, Japanese businessmen still seem to prefer face-to-face communication. They hesitate to discuss important matters over the telephone or send a facsimile message mainly because they feel it is impolite to talk over the telephone or send an impersonal written message and because they simply do not trust a telephone conversation or the written word alone.

If a facsimile is used, the Japanese usually make a phone call first and tell the other party that a message is coming, then call again later to discuss the message over the phone. This is an apparent effort to make the impersonal facsimile message more personal, although the phone call seems wasteful.

Japanese businessmen value the use of all five human senses. In addition, they rely even more heavily on their sixth sense *(kan)* or "intuition" in interpersonal communication. A popular saying often quoted among them is *"Icho o kikeba jū o shiru"* or "Knowing ten hearing only one"—meaning that an astute businessman "is expected to have studied enough to understand a response from contextual information, rather than needing to ask directly."[2] Indeed, to the Japanese, *kan* is another means of communication. In other words, they feel that they need to have face-to-face contacts to obtain "true meanings" from nonverbal aspects such as the vocal tone, facial expression, gestures, and body movement of the other business associates in interpreting what has been communicated.

Meanings in Communications

Generally speaking, Westerners depend heavily on language symbols, and they tend to forget that meanings of words are learned and personal. In other words, they fail to recognize that people attach meanings to the words they use based on their personal experience and that people can communicate with one another only to the extent that they share the same or similar experience.

For example, to an American businessman, the word "urgent" means that he must take action immediately. But to a Japanese businessman, it may mean that he will be required to take action within a few days. A colloquial American English expression, such as "put it on the back burner," is difficult to understand for a Japanese businessman who has never lived in the United States. On the other hand, *Hai, wakarimashita* or "Yes, I understand" uttered frequently by the Japanese businessman may not mean that he is understanding, agreeing, or approving. It might simply mean, "I hear what you are saying." Clearly, some meanings are neither transmittable nor transferable across cultures. Good intercultural communicators must learn to look for what has been communicated, not simply what has been said.

Many Western businesspeople also seem to suffer from the fallacy of "I told you." They assume that what is being told or written to the Japanese business associates once should be understood without difficulties. They fail to realize that all nonnative speakers of English, including the Japanese, need to hear or read the message in English and then translate it into Japanese before they can understand it. This fallacy can become a serious problem in intercultural interpersonal communication. Telling or writing something does not always guarantee that the intended message has been accurately communicated. One effective way to overcome this problem is to have a follow-up telephone call. For example, an American executive who has sent an important letter in English to his Japanese counterpart and has not received any reply for more than a week should call the Japanese executive to check whether or not any words, phrases, or paragraphs in the letter need to be explained.

Sales Presentation

Many international businessmen have had difficulties selling to Japan. Despite strong political pressures from the United States government and other foreign governments, Japan has not really opened its doors to foreign products and services as yet. Many American businesses have been unsuccessful at selling to Japan, as they do not have the determination, the know-how, and the patience to succeed. As a consequence, Japan has had a huge trade surplus with the United States since the 1970s.

One reason why international businessmen, particularly American businessmen, have not fared well in selling to Japan is that they do not know the techniques of "culturally acceptable salesmanship." Japanese techniques differ from American in attitudes, manners, strategies, and the language of sales presentations.

Salesman's Attitude

In Japan, a salesman takes the attitude of subservience and of humility toward his client, of whom he is asking a "big favor." He is very polite, and he is even willing to take some verbal abuse from his client. He is expected to wait patiently for a long time even when he has a confirmed appointment. This attitude comes from the superior status ascribed to the buyer. Whatever knowledge and skills he might have, he will never behave as a proud professional, but as a sincere, even humble, performer of services and favors that the client seeks.[3] He is also the focal point of the sale and must personally attend to most of the problems, including technical ones, instead of having other specialists handle them.

In contrast, an American salesman has the attitude that all business transactions should bring mutual benefit to both the seller and the buyer, and that their relationship is more or less egalitarian. For example, when he sells computer chips at a competitive price, he believes that the buyer will realize a good profit by using them. Consequently, his attitude is more aggressive and demanding and his manner far less apologetic than that of the Japanese salesman. He expects his client to keep the appointment with him. He openly shows his disappointment and displeasure if he is not treated with courtesy and respect. Even many American salesmen who have worked for a while in Japan report that they were frequently angered by the Japanese way of treating a salesman, despite knowing that this is simply a reflection of the status-oriented Japanese society. The American salesman who wishes to be successful in selling in Japan will have to take a less aggressive and less demanding attitude.

Gift of Acquaintance

Presenting a gift to a prospective client on the first visit is a well established social custom among Japanese businessmen. It is called *ochikazuki no shirushi* or "a token gift of acquaintance" and is not considered a bribe in Japan. Unlike American companies, Japanese companies do not have a specific written policy that instructs their executives, managers, or employees not to accept any gift intended to influence purchasing decisions. Even if they have such a policy, they do not strictly enforce it unless a gift is so outrageously expensive that it will result in misuse of managerial prerogative by its recipient. However, there is an unwritten rule called *teido mondai* or "matter of degree," which means, "You can receive a moderate number of gifts, but you will be reprimanded if you receive too much and too often." In other words, every Japanese businessman should know the blurred but critical line between a bribe and a token gift of acquaintance. Although international businessmen might feel that the gift giving imposes unnecessary expense and might frown upon the practice as a shady one or a bribe to curry favor from the person in charge, they cannot ignore this custom entirely when selling to the Japanese.

The type and the value of a gift communicate sincerity and appreciation. The Japanese are very careful in choosing a proper gift; a gift that is either too small or too extravagant will insult the prospective client. International businessmen should consult with their Japanese introducer when choosing an appropriate gift. They can also go to the gift section of a Japanese department store and ask a salesperson for advice. The gift of acquaintance can be a silk necktie, a dozen golf balls, a bottle of Scotch whisky, or a carton of cigarettes.

Get-Acquainted Time

Another apparent difference is that of the length of "get-acquainted time" needed before a serious business discussion takes place. In Japan, businessmen drink tea and engage in small talk by exchanging personal information and discussing current international news, the weather, and similar topics. If they wish to discuss business immediately, they usually apologize by saying, *Sassoku shigoto no ohanashide mōshiwake gozaimasen ga* . . . or "I am sorry that I have to rush into the business discussion right away, but . . ." This apology is a unique Japanese custom; Western businessmen feel no need to engage in a lengthy social conversation and to apologize for bringing up business matters immediately. After all, both parties know that they are getting together for a business discussion. However, Japanese businessmen may not even allow an aggressive salesman to make his sales presentation if they feel that he has violated this important protocol. In some instances, they will intentionally digress to the social conversation again by asking him questions totally unrelated to the business at hand.

What an American salesman has to do, then, is to learn both verbal and nonverbal cues that signal the message from his Japanese client, "Now we can talk business." The Japanese client may say, *Konkai no goyōken wa* . . . or "Your business this time is . . ." Or he may give out subtle nonverbal cues such as keeping silent for a few minutes, having brief eye contact with the salesman, or asking if he needs another cup of tea. Being patient and sensitive is, indeed, a very important step for a salesman trying to establish personal credibility in Japan.

Soft-sell Approach

The initial approach is another critical step in determining the success or failure of any sales presentation. The Japanese sales approach is almost always a "soft sell" rather than a "hard sell." This is again based on the commonly accepted business philosophy in Japan that the buyer is king. The Japanese generally dislike the typical American approach of logical reasoning and aggressive tactics to persuade the prospective client. One common mistake that an American salesman makes in Japan is that he "blows his own horn" too loudly. He talks as if he is the most trustworthy salesman in the world, the product he is selling is the best, and nobody else can supply it at his price. He will run through his professional achievements and explain the merits of buying his product without giving the Japanese client a chance to respond. If the client does not respond immediately, he may even "lecture" on the merits of buying now. Such aggressive behavior, which is quite common and acceptable in the West, will be looked down upon as very rude behavior in Japan. March aptly summarizes the challenges for the Western seller as follows:

> Extrovert, stereotyped salespeople may find it a little more challenging than usual to manage introverted, skeptical, unfriendly Japanese buyers. The Japanese disdain of salesmanship, if you do launch out into product rhetoric, may be offensive. . . . In particular, you may need to speak less, use or tolerate silence more, give your Japanese buyer more personal space (don't physically crowd him), expect that he knows his job (even if on first sight he does not inspire with confidence), and is only doing what he must do, and don't expect to become friends, or even friendly, too quickly."[4]

The salesman should not push too hard from the beginning in a "typical American way" because doing so will make it hard for him to establish rapport with the Japanese.

Offensive Sales Tactics

Common sales tactics used in the Western business context—such as "Never take 'No' for an answer," the "Yes, but" technique, the "Take it or leave it," threat, and the reliance on "the printed word"—are considered very offensive in Japan. Westerners, especially Americans, are taught competition and persistence from an early age and urged not to fear confrontation in interpersonal dealings. In sports, classrooms, or business, they are trained to be aggressive and win at all costs. The following are possible Japanese reactions to these tactics:

"Never Take 'No' for an Answer"

For example, an American salesman who receives "no" will immediately begin to argue and try to change this "no" into "yes." He fails to realize that no matter how logical and plausible his argument might be, he will never persuade a Japanese buyer because in

Japan, an aggressive and argumentative man is never trusted. It is also true that so-called logical truth will not be readily accepted. Kobayashi explains that "the Japanese have a deep-rooted suspicion of what is clearly defined or stated. They believe truth is in the gray zone."[5] Consequently, it is not wise to ask too many "why" and "how-come" questions and to insist on clear answers if the Japanese buyer is unwilling to comply. A common Japanese reaction to such a salesman will be *Kare wa totemo rikuttsuppoi* or "He is too argumentative."

"Yes, But" Technique

This technique also sounds too argumentative to the Japanese buyer. What it actually means is, "Yes, you may be right, but you will change your mind if you listen to my reasoning." In the status-oriented Japanese society, it is always discourteous to argue with anyone who has a higher status—and a buyer always has a higher status. Argument clearly violates the widely accepted philosophy of Japanese businessmen that the customer is always right. The salesman can offend his Japanese client if he keeps on using this technique.

"Take It or Leave It"

This is a high-handed technique to force the Japanese side to agree with the proposition or forget the deal altogether. When selling to the Japanese, it is not a good tactic. Not only will it destroy an amicable interpersonal relationship, but it also provides no flexibility. Quite often, an impatient Western salesman may try to pressure the Japanese to accept an offer by saying, "If you won't take this final offer, I guess I'll have to deal with one of your competitors. That company seems to be very interested in doing business with us." Such a statement will be taken as a threat and will offend and anger the Japanese buyer. Moreover, he will lose face in front of his fellow businessmen.

"The Printed Word"

This tactic uses a voluminous written document in English to overwhelm a Japanese buyer. An unethical salesman can cleverly use this strategy, knowing that it will take the Japanese buyer days to read and translate all the pages of the document. To get the sales contract signed quickly—the salesman's intent—he assures that it is "a standard contract." He even promises that the terms of the contract can be changed later, when in fact the contract is written in his favor and is made legally binding by the Japanese buyer's signature. Many Japanese businessmen are prone to be trapped by this sales tactic because they usually do not consult an attorney before signing a contract.

These offensive tactics may bring quick profits to the clever salesman who uses them, but he will never be able to establish a long-term business relationship with the Japanese.

Proper Steps in Sales Presentations

There are six different steps in a sales presentation: approach, attention, need, satisfaction, close, and follow-up. Each of these steps must be planned and executed properly with good knowledge of their cultural implications.

Approach

Even though an appointment has been made a few weeks in advance, it is always wise to reconfirm it the day or even a few hours before the appointment. The client may be out of town on an emergency business trip and the appointment will have to be rescheduled, especially if he is a busy executive. It is also important to check how much time it will take to get to his office (and to factor in such variables as traffic congestion or missed train connections). It is advisable not to take a taxi during morning and afternoon rush hours, when traffic can be terrible in big Japanese cities such as Tokyo, Yokohama, and Osaka.

Upon arrival at the Japanese client's office, a foreign businessman must first check with the receptionist. The visitor is usually expected to wait until a male assistant comes and escorts him to a conference room. The person escorting the visitor will indicate which seat he should occupy, and the secretary will bring a cup of Japanese green tea or coffee for him and another cup for her manager. The visitor should not drink the tea until the host comes and offers it to him.★ When the Japanese client comes in, the visitor should stand up, shake hands, and exchange *meishi*. Then, they sit down to chat and try to establish rapport by engaging in small talk for a while. This process relaxes both men psychologically before they begin a serious business discussion.

Attention

Transition to attention is not easy; the salesman must analyze the prospective client's mood to determine whether he should continue to engage in informal chitchat or get down to business right away. If the Japanese client seems ready to talk business, the salesman humbly presents information regarding the company's recent business activities with an annual report and other printed materials. Important data and information should be presented on overhead transparencies or on flip charts. Many foreign companies ignore the importance of having these items of corporate information translated into Japanese. Knowing that most Japanese businessmen understand English, they feel that they can get by with only English. However, they must realize that Japanese is still the language of business transactions in Japan. Besides, using Japanese will create a strong impression that his company is serious about doing business with the Japanese client and will draw favorable attention to the company's image, credibility, and reliability.

Need

Once the prospective client is convinced that he should listen to the sales presentation, the salesman can begin to discuss his specific proposal. He must find out what his client's needs are by tactfully asking questions. Often a Western businessman does not listen carefully to what is being said and instead rushes to explain his proposal. He should be patient and slow down, and wait for reactions to each point of his presentation. Generally speaking, the Japanese

---

★ This is not a cup of coffee or tea offered to a visitor to drink while waiting in a typical American business context. In Japan, the visitor should not help himself before he is offered it by the host.

do not respond immediately like Westerners, and they do not voice objections quickly. Based on what he has found out, the salesman must clearly identify specific needs and try to meet them at the client's request.

Satisfaction

Once the needs are well defined, the salesman must satisfy them by providing a specific proposal or sales contract. The prospective buyer may have questions about price, quality, delivery, payment, service, warranty, advertising allowance, and so on. The salesman needs to be prepared to answer all of these questions satisfactorily. In this step, the salesman should emphasize the benefits and advantages of doing business with him so that the client can visualize what this business transaction will bring him and his company. The salesman should know that the Japanese are very meticulous and demanding of good service and on-time delivery. At this stage, the salesman's ability to make a firm commitment on the spot is very important. An excuse like "I'll have to check on that with the home office" will never help him close a business deal in Japan.

Close

The close is the most difficult part of any sales presentation because the salesman must initiate it. It is even more difficult to close a sale with the Japanese, who are extremely reluctant to make a final purchasing commitment on the spot. After having seemed agreeable all along the way, they may suddenly become vague and evasive. There are two reasons for this behavior: (1) The person who has been listening to the sales presentation is not the real decision maker. (2) One individual executive or manager cannot make a commitment, even though he might have been personally persuaded. In Japanese business organizations almost all major decisions are made by consensus. Consequently, too aggressive an approach may backfire on a salesman. If he tries too hard to push a sale, he may get a "reluctant yes" which really means "no." Instead of pushing, he must explain or answer questions fairly and tactfully until the Japanese side feels psychologically comfortable and ready to accept the proposed sales contract.

At this stage, an aggressive American salesman, assuming that the sale is made, is likely to ask, "Which payment schedule would you prefer—a thirty-day net or a sixty-day credit plan?" instead of saying, "If you want to buy this product, I will offer you two payment plans." This technique seems to work well with an American client who needs a little push, but it will not work well with the Japanese. They may feel offended by this sales trick.

In most instances, they will say, "I'll call you later when we decide." The salesman should not readily accept this answer, because the chances are they will never call back. He must politely insist that he needs to know when he can call back for a definite answer. If he cannot get any positive indication of their willingness to do business, he should stop chasing the Japanese client.

Follow-up

When the sale is concluded, the salesman should tactfully reassure the client that he has made a wise decision with such statements as "I'm sure that you made the right decision," "We won't be able to offer this product at the same price next month," and "I'm sure that you will have a lot of satisfied customers." The salesman can send a letter of appreciation to the client and/or make a telephone call and offer further assistance. He might say, "Mr. Tanaka, I called to thank you for the order you gave me yesterday. Please call me if you need any more assistance. It was indeed a pleasure doing business with your esteemed company." Good follow-up always assures the client that he made the right decision and also helps him rationalize his action. In other words, it is insurance against the client's reversing his decision.

c h a p t e r **5**

Contract Negotiation and Conflict Resolution

Negotiating contracts and resolving disputes across cultural and linguistic barriers require good cultural knowledge, better communication skills, and a great deal of patience and perseverance. Negotiators, mediators, and arbitrators must understand how culture and language affect the process and the outcome of their efforts. Despite the fact that Japanese multinational corporations are engaging in business activities all over the world, Japanese businessmen still use their unique culture-bound ways, especially when it comes to contract negotiation and conflict resolution. Many foreign businesspeople find that the negotiation tactics of seemingly amicable Japanese businessmen are unbusinesslike, ambiguous, insincere, and even deceitful.

Japan is an Asian country, but the Japanese style of negotiation is very different from negotiation styles in China and Korea, Japan's closest Asian neighbors. In contrast to the aggressive haggling typical of Chinese and Koreans, the Japanese prefer to engage in more subtle and low-keyed bargaining.[1] The vertical nature of Japanese society, which places a high value on saving face and avoiding interpersonal confrontations, has also discouraged the Japanese from adopting the American style of aggressive bargaining and confrontation. It goes without saying that a good understanding of unique Japanese ways is the most important prerequisite for successful dealings with the Japanese.

Negotiation

Negotiating with the Japanese can be a difficult and frustrating experience for Westerners and other Asians alike. The attitudes of Japanese negotiators toward negotiation and their distinctive negotiation tactics are based on the traditional Japanese business culture and social customs. To begin with, the word "negotiation" and its usual Japanese translation, *kōshō* have significantly different meanings. Whereas "negotiation" usually suggests discussion, concession, and conference in the Western culture, *kōshō* has nuances in Japanese of fighting, conflict, strategy, argument, and debate. Consequently, the Japanese frequently enter into negotiation sessions expecting to be given a hard time, and they feel that they must arm themselves in advance.[2] The Japanese are also not accustomed to negotiating a contract according to an itemized agenda. They prefer to solve contractual issues or problems through informal *hanashiai* or a series of "mutual consultations" away from a negotiation table. They are usually not concerned about specific items of the contract under consideration, but about first reaching a broad agreement by establishing a trusting relationship between the two parties. They always want to establish a warm *ningen kankei* or "interpersonal relationship" rather than a rigid contractual obligation to one another. Some Japanese businessmen are even willing to enter into a contract without carefully checking its details when they find their business associates to be warm *(atatakai)* and sincere *(seijitsu)*.

Despite the rapid Westernization of Japanese society during the past several decades, Japan's historical and cultural roots still influence the Japanese negotiation style. As we have seen, the Tokugawa shogunate successfully maintained self-imposed seclusion from direct foreign contacts for more than 250 years (1616–1867). During this period, Japan's population became very homogenous, and the Japanese people developed their unique culture and social customs. Because rice farming was the most important economic activity in Japan for many centuries, rice-farming culture persists in a modified form even in today's industrialized Japan. Unlike the individualistic hunting and gathering culture of the West, rice farming in Japan required close cooperation and the participation of many groups of families and friends from the village. Rice cultivation taught the Japanese to de-emphasize individual needs and desires in favor of group interests. This attitude of group-centeredness and mutual assistance is still perpetuated in schools and at workplaces in Japan. In addition, the small and mountainous geography of Japan and the dense population have influenced the Japanese to think of others' needs and feelings in social interactions and business dealings. In classrooms, lively discussions are not part of the Japanese students' experience. Quiet listening and obedience are rewarded rather than debating skills and independent thinking. Likewise, Japanese businessmen are not rewarded for their eloquence and verbal skills. They almost always avoid the combative or debating style of negotiation often used by American businessmen. Talkativeness is also considered a negative trait for a respectable Japanese businessman.

Another important influence on Japanese negotiating style is that Japan is a vertically structured society based on the traditional teaching of Confucius. At the interpersonal level, age, sex, education, occupation, and relationship are the bases of status distinction. People at all levels feel uncomfortable if status distinctions are ignored in interpersonal interactions. These status distinctions also affect how participants behave in business negotiations. Consequently, the Japanese always play a "status game," while the Westerners may go out of their way to establish interpersonal equality.

It is crucial to understand why and how the Japanese negotiate the way they do. There are several important considerations and effective tactics for successful negotiations with the Japanese.

Preparing for Negotiation

To prepare for effective negotiation, one must (1) determine the purpose of the negotiation; (2) assess the situation; (3) select appropriate negotiation team members; (4) gather pertinent information and data; (5) make an agenda; and (6) work out concession strategies.

The type and scope of preparation needed for determining the purpose of the negotiation hinges on whether it is a new

contract negotiation or renegotiation of an old contract. If it is for
a new contract, it is only necessary to provide a lot of information
and materials to impress the prospective Japanese business associates. On the other hand, if it is a renegotiation, it is necessary to
provide new information and data that will help renegotiate the
specific terms of the existing contract.

The second step is to assess the situation accurately. It is
essential to assess the relative power relationship first. A large
and powerful Japanese company can be more demanding than a
medium-sized or a small company. The buyer-seller relationship
is another important factor. As we have seen, in Japan's business
world, buyers always outrank sellers. March explains, "Among the
Japanese, this difference in status is clearly marked by the deferen-
tial behavior of the seller, who uses honorific language, and con-
versely, by the mildly haughty manners of the buyer."[3] This means
that the Japanese buyer unilaterally controls the way the negotiation proceeds and expects much more respect and deference from
the seller. On the other hand, if the Japanese side is selling, the
Japanese negotiators will act with humility and utmost courtesy. It
is also important to recognize that some Japanese companies value
the prestige of doing business with a big and famous multinational company over short-term profitability.

The third step is to carefully select the negotiation team
members. Most Western businessmen, especially American executives, feel that they should be able to handle any negotiation single-handedly. This "I can go it alone" attitude can be a severe
disadvantage; a single negotiator will be outnumbered by a larger
Japanese negotiation team whose members are assigned specific
tasks. No matter how talented a person might be, one American
executive can hardly follow several things that are going on during
a negotiation session.

It is also very important to match ranks of those who are
selected to participate. If a senior vice president, vice president of
the international department, and director of marketing are expected to come from the Japanese side, the American side should send
executives of the same rank to the negotiation table. It is an utmost
insult to the Japanese if young, junior American managers are
assigned to represent their company in Japan. Unfortunately, women
and minority executives are not eagerly accepted in Japan's business circles as bona fide representatives as yet.

As for characteristics of a good bargainer, Graham and Sano claim that those characteristics identified by American executives such as thinking under pressure, product knowledge, and verbal skills are of secondary importance in Japanese negotiations. They suggest that listening ability, interpersonal orientation, willingness to use team assistance, self-esteem, high aspirations, attractiveness, and influence at headquarters are particularly important when negotiating with the Japanese.[4] Listening ability is especially critical when negotiating across cultural and linguistic barriers. It may be difficult for Westerners to accurately understand what Japanese negotiators are explaining in poor English unless they listen patiently and pay very close attention.* Interpersonal orientation means that bargainers take a flexible approach instead of stubbornly clinging to their culture-bound ways of negotiating. They should be able to "play the chameleon" if the situation requires it. Willingness to use team assistance is not a trait that most Americans will cherish, but it makes a substantial difference in international negotiation, particularly when negotiating with team-oriented Japanese negotiators. Not only does the team approach alleviate the burden on the one or two individuals in charge, but the inclusion of several technical or financial experts in the team also helps establish personal relationships with their Japanese counterparts. Self-esteem or belief in one's own ideas is an important personal asset because negotiators are often required to work and act in ambiguous situations without the benefit of having the immediate help of their superiors and subordinates. They are also required to bridge the gap between their home office and the Japanese business associates.

High aspirations regarding the deal to be negotiated are important. Negotiators must show their enthusiasm and long-term commitment personally if they hope to gain respect and support from their Japanese counterparts. This does not mean that negotiators ought to be peppy and talkative, but they need to show sincere interest and enthusiasm. In addition, negotiators should be refined, courteous, and intelligent people who are not ethnocen-

---

* Not all Japanese negotiators speak "broken English," but they may not speak logically and coherently like Westerners because they are usually translating Japanese thoughts into English.

tric and are free of racial prejudice. In Japan, *ningensei* or "humanness" is considered a more important trait than business acumen. The Japanese feel more comfortable doing business with "friends" rather than with calculating business partners.★

Influence at headquarters is a particularly important characteristic. For international businessmen, the toughest part of their negotiations in a foreign country is selling the agreement to headquarters. Because they understand the situation much better than the people at headquarters, they are frequently compelled to make proper concessions based on their own judgment. However, they are often criticized for not presenting the home office's view strongly enough and for making unnecessary concessions. Therefore, it is critical that the negotiators selected to represent the company have real influence at headquarters so that they can effectively negotiate and successfully implement the fruits of their effort. If it is necessary to hire an interpreter, it is always advisable to hire a professional interpreter instead of asking the Japanese side to provide the interpreting service. Finally, it is best not to include legal counsel on the initial negotiation team unless legal opinions are absolutely necessary during the negotiation. The presence of lawyers can cause uneasiness and suspicion among the Japanese negotiation team members. Japanese companies usually have their secretariat office *(bunsho ka)*, not lawyers, draw up contracts and agreements. They hire lawyers only when they need to solve legal disputes.

The fourth step in negotiation preparation is to gather specific pertinent information and data. It is absolutely necessary to learn as much as possible about a potential Japanese business partner through their corporate pamphlets, recent stock market reports, and trade newspapers and journals. The investigation should include information regarding the company's market share, ranking within its industry, financial status, and plans for future expansion. In addition to getting background information on those who are actually participating in the negotiation sessions,

---

★ Japanese businessmen often complain that Westerners, particularly Americans, are too focused on the logical, rational, and legal aspects of contract negotiation and ignore the emotional, intuitive, and human aspects of establishing business relationships.

it is necessary to obtain personal background information about the key executives of the company through the Japanese "Who's Who" books and informal sources.* In Japan, it must be remembered that *who* is involved is more important than *what* is being done in any business transaction, and knowing a lot about key executives will make a good impression on the Japanese negotiation team members. It is also necessary to know the Japanese company's group affiliation *(keiretsu)* and a main bank that the company has been dealing with. In many instances, representatives of both the parent company and the main bank will participate in an important negotiation as observers.

The fifth step is to work out an agenda. One side can prepare the agenda or both sides can do it jointly. It is more prudent to work it out jointly through a series of informal sessions because Japanese negotiators dislike surprises. The agenda should list all issues to be negotiated. To prevent time from being wasted on minor issues, major issues should be listed first. However, if the major issues are expected to cause serious difficulties, the minor ones should be listed first so that negotiators can handle the easy-to-handle issues early in the process. Mutual concessions on the minor issues, in turn, could build an atmosphere of goodwill and cooperation, and at the same time, these concessions could be used to balance concessions on the major issues. It is always wise to prepare two agendas: a general agenda to be presented to the other side and a detailed agenda for one's own use. The latter includes detailed notes and a contingency strategies about what to do at each step of the way. It is also necessary to recognize that the Japanese may not stick to the agenda and discuss each item sequentially as Americans generally do. They often deviate from the agenda when they find it difficult to follow and return to a particular agenda item later. The key is to be flexible and not to insist on strictly following the agenda.

The sixth step—to work out concession strategies—is the most difficult step for American negotiators. They commonly make

---

* In some instances, other foreign companies that have dealt with that Japanese company can be valuable sources of information, but they might also provide biased and subjective information. A reliable introducer can also be a valuable source of information.

the following mistakes: They make unnecessary concessions along the way, assuming that the Japanese side will reciprocate. They also believe that concession on each agenda item will lead to a quick conclusion of the negotiation. Another mistake is caused by impatience and an inclination to "split the difference" when the negotiation bogs down; the Japanese often play on this impatience and generosity of the Americans to gain an advantage. Still another mistake is that American team members openly argue among themselves in front of their Japanese counterparts. It would be better to take breaks and caucus whenever they have disagreements. The Japanese side will use intrateam disputes to try to put a wedge between the American team members and take advantage of an unsettling situation. Japanese negotiators never make a concession or reconsider anything without first taking a break and reaching a consensus among themselves.

Manipulation of Situational Factors

Once preparations for negotiation are completed, negotiators must consider situational factors such as where the negotiations are to be held, time limits, and playing on audiences.

The location of the negotiations can be the most important situational factor. It has both practical and psychological implications on the process and the outcome of negotiation. If the negotiation is held in one's own territory, the home team will have "home court advantage": (1) The home team members have access to all the necessary information and resources close by. (2) They can get approval or disapproval on the problems that they did not anticipate. (3) They can take care of other business matters and have their own facilities available while handling the negotiations. (4) They can obtain additional assistance from their support groups in collecting necessary data and materials for the ongoing negotiation. (5) They have the psychological advantage of having the other side come to them. (6) They can save traveling time and avoid paying long-distance telephone charges.

Having the negotiation held in the opponent's territory also has some advantages: (1) The visiting team members can devote their full attention to the on-going negotiation without interruptions from their offices. (2) They can withhold information or commitment, stating that they have to ask the home office. (4) They may have the option of going over their opponent's head to an executive with a higher managerial position in the latter's company if no satisfactory answers are forthcoming. (5) The burden of preparation is on the other side.

Deciding on the location is particularly important when negotiating with the Japanese because they always want to gain the psychological advantage over the visiting foreigners. They are quite willing to spend a large sum of money for their guests' entertainment to gain this advantage. They might say, "Tokyo is lovely this time of year. Cherry trees will be in full bloom. You can do some sightseeing while you are on this trip." This is one of their tactics to manipulate the negotiation setting. The visitors should not be too willing to accept lavish entertainment and should avoid becoming too obligated to the Japanese host (although it is impolite and undiplomatic to give a flat refusal). The visitors should also be cautious not to mistake this Japanese hospitality for friendship; it is simply standard practice.[5] If possible, it is a good idea to cancel out the obligation by countering with a similar invitation. For example, the visiting American negotiators can host an American-style dinner party at their hotel in exchange for the geisha party hosted by the Japanese side.

If neither side is willing to give in on the location, it is a good idea to suggest a neutral location like Hawai'i. In addition to having beautiful beaches and golf courses, Hawai'i is a convenient location for consummating many trans-Pacific business deals. At any rate, bargaining over location is best handled in a subtle and indirect manner through informal talks.

If it is necessary to travel to Japan, however, one can reduce the home court advantage of the Japanese side. One good strategy is to hold meetings at your hotel conference room and invite the Japanese negotiation team to call on you. It is also wise to pay for restaurant and bar expenses instead of having the Japanese side pay for everything.

Time limits are another extremely critical factor to be considered. *Toki wa kanenari* or "Time is money" is a common saying among Japanese businessmen, but they do not handle time in the same efficient way as Westerners do. They become very cautious and are willing to take lots more time when it comes to an international business negotiation. They also play a status game by manipulating time usage and thereby testing the patience of busy

Westerners, particularly Americans, to the limit. In fact, many American businesspeople complain bitterly that the clock moves much more slowly in Japan.

The Japanese side may intentionally delay a decision for no apparent reasons to squeeze out concessions when the American side pushes to consummate a deal. Japan-bound American businesspeople are often advised not to tell the Japanese side their scheduled departure from Japan because they will be taken advantage of if they reveal a rushed time schedule. A longer stay in Japan will communicate a strong message of commitment, which in turn, will influence the Japanese negotiators' behavior during the negotiation sessions. In some instances, American religious or national holidays are used as a lever. Obviously, it is not a good idea to allow the Japanese side to schedule a difficult negotiation right before Easter, Thanksgiving, or Christmas because they know that American businesspeople will rush home to spend the holidays with their families. It is also unwise to schedule negotiation sessions in Japan during long Japanese holidays. For example, Japanese offices close during three long annual holidays: the Golden Week (April 29 through May 5), Obon (Buddhist holidays—August 15 through 17), and New Year's holidays (December 27 through January 5). Still another consideration in scheduling negotiation sessions is that the fiscal calendar for Japanese businesses and government offices begins in April and ends in March.

Playing on audiences can be an effective strategy with the Japanese, but only if it is orchestrated well. Japanese businessmen are so concerned about a good corporate image that they can be pressured into taking actions based on this concern rather than on practical business concerns. Under certain circumstances, they may even overlook obvious disadvantages or minor problems and conclude a business deal just to uphold the public image of their company. The Japanese are sensitive to international and local mass media, competitors, their main banks, government ministries, trade associations, and the general public. Today, a news scoop on a large-scale Japan-U.S. business transaction that is being negotiated can influence its outcome. It is difficult then for either party to deny the already publicized agreement or business venture. Since Japanese corporations must face keen competition from domestic rivals, they are extremely mindful of what their competitors will think if they cannot consummate the publicized deal. They sometimes take hasty actions just to show off to their competitors. In fact, this "me-too" attitude caused floods of direct capital invest-ments from Japan into U.S. real estate markets during the eco-nomic bubble years of the late 1980s.

According to Van Zandt, foreign businessmen find that there are three parties when they negotiate in Japan: the Japanese company, the foreign company, and the Japanese government.[6] The negotiation will be several times more difficult when the gov-ernment participates even indirectly. At times, the government may play a face-saving role and deny the application for licensing or opening a new foreign venture if the Japanese company wants to back out of an agreement already reached. Sometimes, the Japanese company's bank will also become another party to the negotiation, although the bank representative will not participate in actual negotiation sessions. Trade associations also apply pressure to pre-vent introduction of new foreign businesses or products that will negatively affect the status quo of Japan's domestic market. For example, strong political pressure from trade associations kept large foreign discount stores and foreign rice, apples, oranges, and beef out of Japan until very recently. Although the Japanese public has had a stronger voice in recent years and advocates introducing for-eign products, Japanese consumers do not have enough power to help eliminate the direct or indirect restrictions on the importation of foreign products. Foreign businesspeople must learn to manipu-late these audiences to their advantage if they wish to carry out successful business negotiations in Japan.

Understanding Unique Negotiation Tactics

Several Japanese negotiation tactics may be considered unethical and unacceptable in the Western business context. One such tactic is to gain psychological advantage over the opponent by deception. March claims that Japanese negotiators still follow the advice of Sun Tsu, a fourth-century Chinese militarist, on the art of war: "To defeat the enemy psychologically is the superior strategy. The war-rior's way is one of deception. The key to success is to capitalize upon your power to do the unexpected, when appearing to be unprepared."[7] To implement this tactic, Japanese negotiators patiently conduct "intelligence work." In addition to formally requesting written materials, they will make an extra effort to obtain more information via informal means before negotiating. A Japanese manager in charge may suggest playing a game of golf or having a nice dinner, and he will not spare expense or stint on time for these tasks. Then he will nonchalantly ask a member of the other side's negotiating team what he thinks about the upcoming contract, top management's attitude, the urgency of the pending deal, existence of competitors, and the like.

Other Japanese negotiation tactics include padded offers, contingent offers, shifting blame, victim mentality, indulgent dependency, emotion-drenched personal appeal, and maintaining interpersonal harmony.

Japanese negotiators routinely use padded offers when they do not know what to expect from foreign buyers or sellers, as they feel it is safer to leave room to maneuver. Japanese merchants frequently use *Kama o kakeru* (trying to draw out true intentions by making an outrageous offer) when bargaining for price a reduction. Westerners become suspicious if the Japanese, after making an outrageous offer and justifying it, shamelessly change it to a more realistic one when they encounter a strong objection. This tactic is a stark contrast to the American negotiators' straightforward and honest disclosure of information. The Western tactic of saying, "You tell me what you want, and I'll tell you what we want," will not work in Japan.

"You go first" or the contingent offer is a tactic frequently used by the Japanese. They will never disclose their own negotiating positions first without knowing the opponents' positions. In other words, they will make concessions or compromises only if the opponents do so first. The Japanese abhor making unilateral concessions or "giving up something for nothing."[8] If they are forced to make a concession, they will, to save face, demand at least a token concession in return.

Shifting the blame onto the other side is another face-saving device almost always used by the Japanese whenever negotiations bog down. Historically, the Japanese have always blamed foreigners whenever they had to face up to serious international conflicts.[9] This tendency is based on the sense of rightness rooted in the widespread conviction that the Japanese are, as a race, decent, honorable, and innocent people. The most common form of blame is attacking the lack of *sei'i* (sincerity) of the opposing party. The assumption is that any problems could be solved if the opponent were sincere and willing to cooperate. This argument is based on their subjective assessment of the situation rather than an objective analysis of the data and information.[10]

Another Japanese attitude is *higaisha ishiki* or "victim mentality." "When the Japanese are threatened or attacked by others, they see it immediately as unfair. They see themselves as weak, defenseless, and victimized."[11] Because of this attitude, the Japanese are unyielding and will refuse to make any concessions even under strong foreign pressure. Japan's response to the continued bashing about unfair trade practices by American political and business leaders takes the form of victim mentality. The Japanese people feel that Japan has been made a scapegoat by the United States and Asian countries for economic, political, and even social problems. For this reason, they have a strong tendency to blame the other side when negotiations become deadlocked or break off. They may complain to the other side by saying, "American negotiators are too demanding and have no patience at all. We could reach an agreement if they were reasonable and understanding of Japan's situation."

A uniquely Japanese negotiation tactic is the use of *amae* or "indulgent dependency" in negotiating with a more powerful opponent. In Japan-U.S. trade negotiations, the Japanese government continues to use *amae* to appeal for understanding of Japan's "fragile status" and asks generosity of the "powerful" United States. Lebra explains that this use of *amae* is a form of status manipulation. "It is not uncommon that a Japanese negotiator, apparently without bargaining power, succeeds in negotiation entirely by humbling himself, by bowing low and begging persistently."[12] He succeeds by causing the other party to feel guilty for keeping him in such a shameful posture. In the Japanese cultural context, this humble posture has a strong persuasive appeal. When a person of superior status assumes a humble posture and asks for the help of an inferior, his persuasive appeal is overwhelming. In addition, a flat refusal of such a disparate request made by the high-status person at a high cost of face often calls for retaliation in the Japanese social context.

Naniwabushi or an "emotion-drenched personal appeal" is a similar emotional device to arouse empathy. The origin of *naniwabushi* traces back to the stories told by street entertainers that became popular among the common folk during the latter decades

95

of the Tokugawa shogunate. The typical themes were sad plights of broken loves and separated family members, and exploits of *yakuza*★ whose good deeds were glorified. *Naniwabushi* in today's business context refers to making decisions based more on emotional feelings and less on objective reasoning. March explains that *naniwabushi* consists of three phases: the opening *(kikkake)*, which gives the general background of the story and tells what the people involved are thinking or feeling; an account of critical events *(seme)*; and expression of sorrow *(urei)* at what has happened.[13] In some ways, this is very similar to "crying on someone's shoulder." It is still an effective tactic in Japan. Westerners may think that it is not a very persuasive tactic, but they should be aware that the Japanese may use this *naniwabushi* tactic against them. It is reported that this tactic was successfully used by the executive vice president of Allied Import Company of Japan when he had to break the impasse during the final stage of negotiation with Safeway Stores.[14]

Harmony *(wa)* is one of the important cultural values of Japanese society. Japanese negotiators often avoid saying "no" to maintain interpersonal harmony in face-to-face communication. This is in sharp contrast to the candor of American negotiators who might say, "Tell me yes or tell me no—but give me a straight answer."[15] Consequently, American negotiators complain about the difficulties of getting clear feedback from the Japanese negotiators, especially when the negotiation is not going well. Instead of saying "yes" or "no," the Japanese use subtle nonverbal signals such as avoiding eye contact, prolonged silence, and scratching the head. Or they may make ambiguous statements like "It can be very difficult" or "We'll think it over carefully, and let you know our answer later." Both of these statements actually mean, "Our answer is 'no,' but we won't say so because we don't want to cause ill feelings right here."

Japanese negotiators also use the dual approach of *tatemae* (official stance) and *honne* (true mind). In formal negotiation ses-

---

★ *Yakuza* is a criminal element in Japanese society that engages in such illegal activities as extortion, racketeering, loan sharking, drug trafficking, prostitution, and gambling. However, *yakuza* bosses were once revered as kindhearted men and friends of the poor like Robin Hoods of Nottingham during the samurai era of the nineteenth century.

sions, the Japanese will reveal what ought to be said rather than what they really mean. For example, the Japanese company's *tatemae* is that they still wish to make a deal, but the *honne* is that they are no longer interested in the deal. This seems hypocritical, but this is how the Japanese avoid saying "no" in the interest of maintaining interpersonal harmony. The Japanese seem to expect Westerners to understand what they really mean by observing the subtle but clear verbal and nonverbal cues and innuendoes.

On the other hand, *honne* may be expressed directly in some instances. The Japanese will give a "flat no" when they realize that they are in much higher positions in their status relationship with others. For example, an irate Japanese manager of a large company can become very rude and blunt when he talks to a staff member of its foreign subsidiary company. Clear "yes" or "no" answers can be used between close friends and family members when there is no danger of hurting others' feelings.

Conducting the Negotiation

Opening a negotiation session with Japanese negotiators requires a few important social rituals. First, the Japanese side prefers to take a lot more time for *aisatsu* (greeting) and introduction of each member. They may nonchalantly ask questions about both the personal and professional backgrounds of each member of the opposing team. They will engage in nontask-sounding social conversation to find out whether the opposing team members are trustworthy and sincere and have a cooperative attitude. They need to establish an amicable interpersonal relationship and a pleasant atmosphere before getting down to business. They usually spend ten or twenty minutes on this kind of conversation, drinking tea or coffee and chatting.

During this period, a few top Japanese executives may appear for a few minutes just for *aisatsu* and have a cup of tea with the visitors. These executives do not usually participate in the actual negotiation sessions, but their appearance at this time is a clear signal that the Japanese side is serious about the new deal to be negotiated. Their function is mainly ceremonial, and they exchange *meishi* with the visitors and engage in small talk for a few minutes.

They may also pass their intuitive judgment on the visiting nego-tiators and talk about their first impressions to the Japanese nego-tiating team members later.

Once the Japanese negotiators are satisfied with the non-task sounding, they will initiate the discussion of business. It is wise not to rush them into this second stage of negotiation; failure to establish trusting personal relationships with the Japanese negotia-tion team members at this stage may result in misunderstandings, distorted perceptions, hostility, unexpected postponement, and even abandonment of the negotiated deal.

In discussing the agenda items, it is necessary to recognize that the Japanese usually take a holistic approach or nonsequen-tial approach. Graham and Sano label this particular Japanese approach "conversational meanders."[16] The Japanese usually begin with the general issue, talking unsystematically around it and meandering without regard to the agenda or structure. Western businesspeople, who believe that there is a set of issues and that each issue should be settled independently, may be frustrated and annoyed with the lack of a logical sequence. They must play along with the Japanese by being patient and accepting their way of han-dling the agenda items.

At this stage, good communication is a very critical factor. Both of the opposing negotiation teams must perform the follow-ing tasks: (1) find out what settlement their opponent would be willing to accept; (2) reveal to the opponent what settlement would be acceptable to them; (3) influence the opponent by means of persuasion or threat to accept the offer; (4) provide the oppo-nent with justifications for accepting the proposed settlement. These tasks are not easy to accomplish, especially when either party suffers from a language handicap. In negotiating with the Japanese, it is erroneous to assume that every Japanese negotiator has a professional competence in English. Nevertheless, to avoid embarrassment, some of them may not openly admit that they can-not negotiate complex issues in English. Invariably, aggressive American negotiators overwhelm the Japanese side by one-sided logical arguments and strong contentions. Because the Japanese typically show little physical and verbal activity, the Americans, who can easily dominate the verbal interaction, assume that they are winning the negotiation. In reality, however, the Japanese are "being out-talked, not out-negotiated."[17] The typical Japanese reaction to this tactic is to insist that the same points be repeated or to become totally unresponsive.

If they wish to solve this problem, the American negotiators must recognize that it takes more time for the Japanese to respond to questions in English. They should not volunteer to supply words, phrases, and sentences when the Japanese are still struggling to express their thoughts in English. They must learn to allow long pauses and silences without getting frustrated or impatient. They should not use colloquial expressions and should refrain from joking around just to be friendly. If the Japanese negotiators are having difficulty in understanding what has been talked about, the Americans may have to repeat the same explanations a few times. In all instances, written explanation, graphs, figures, pictures, and slides are extremely useful in overcoming communication difficulties. American negotiators should carefully plan their English communication and should allow ample time for questions and clarifications.

During the negotiation, certain "signposts" or verbal and nonverbal messages communicate the parameters within which negotiation can take place. Signposting is used to test each party's strength or weakness and minimum and maximum positions. For example, the Japanese side may strongly object and threaten to cancel the entire negotiation if the American side asks for a large lump-sum payment. From this negative reaction, the American side can perceive that this is a high-risk and tension-raising issue. This signpost warns the Americans that insisting on a large lump-sum payment will be a source of possible conflict.

Effective negotiators need to develop flexible communication strategies to cope with possible conflicts and to look for signposts of "give points" and "must points." Their strategy must be based on prior fact-finding research and informal consultations. They will have to determine what the bargaining issues are and arrange them in order of importance. The less important issues, the "give points," can be used as trade-offs. At the same time, negotiators must find the opponents' "must points," points they will not give away easily. The negotiators must get around those points and try to gain as much as they can. They must also be flexible enough to modify their negotiation strategy if they later find out that the opponents have changed their "must points" or that they themselves inaccurately estimated the opponents' positions.

Avoiding Unacceptable Communication Strategies

All parties involved in negotiation are motivated to compete and cooperate at the same time. While the opposing parties fight for the best attainable position, both parties must work together to reach a mutually acceptable agreement. The ideal result of negotiation should not be "winner take all," but a "win-win situation." However, it is not always possible to conduct amicable negotiation sessions and reach a perfect agreement. In negotiating across cultures, interpersonal conflicts are bound to develop because the parties do not share the same perceptions of what is appropriate and what is inappropriate. The other side has different cultural values, social customs, standards of ethics, and business principles and practices. Ethnocentrism, racial stereotypes, and prejudices become even more critical factors when judging honesty, sincerity, and trustworthiness. Negotiators need to avoid ill-conceived and unscrupulous tactics such as polarized communication, misdirected communication, deceptive communication, and pseudo-logical arguments.

Polarized communication makes the negotiation a win-lose situation. It clearly shows that the opposing positions are miles apart and suggests that a settlement can be reached only at the expense of the other party. It not only creates tension, but it also creates a high-risk situation. In an emotionally charged situation, an American executive may be tempted to behave aggressively as if he were negotiating in the United States and say, "You just take our offer or leave it! Your excuse for not agreeing to it now is totally unacceptable. You are so evasive and too slow in decision making. As you know, we don't have to deal with you. There are many Chinese and Korean companies wanting to jump at this business deal." Such statements make mutual cooperation nearly impossible. They display an ethnocentric attitude and an unwillingness to accept different Japanese business practices. The American negotiator must recognize that the imposition of American ways will invite negative results. What is called "reasonable and proper" in negotiating a contract in the American business context can be offensive in other cultures.

Misdirected communication takes several different forms. One common type is an attempt to make the other party feel guilty. Suppose that a joint venture between an American company and a Japanese company does not work, and a meeting is called to restructure the previous agreement. The American side tries to make the Japanese side feel guilty by openly stating, "We feel that you have not lived up to our agreement. This venture has failed because you did not assign competent managers. You spent too much money for entertainment for nothing. We don't think this negotiation will result in anything worthwhile." This form of misdirected communication makes the Japanese side extremely defensive and angry. The Japanese are quick to take offense even at an unintended slight. They tend to interpret objective observations and constructive criticisms as personal attacks on them and on the whole Japanese race. Some older Japanese still experience feelings of awkwardness or inferiority, and they are easily intimidated when dealing with Westerners.

Deceptive communication is another unethical tactic to gain a strategic advantage over an opponent by exaggeration, fictitious examples, actual lies, or bluffing. These attempts to inflate the bargaining position create serious drawbacks. Once the actual position is known, the deceiving party will be forced to retreat from the inflated position. He will lose credibility and find it difficult to obtain concessions from the other party.

Another common form of deceptive communication is the intentional piling up of small "give points" and issues tangentially related to the main issue. This strategy is designed to overwhelm the opponent by the sheer weight of material presented. It will never be effective, because the opponent will quickly recognize the peripheral nature of those irrelevant materials, discount their importance and question the sincerity of the deceiving party. In today's high-tech information society, it is virtually impossible to deceive an opponent with false information and inflated data. Retrieval and verification of the information and data are easy and instant from every corner of the world.

Pseudo-logical arguments are often used in negotiation by Westerners. American negotiators are especially fond of logical arguments. They have been taught to defend their contentions by asserting themselves at home, at school, and at work. They tend to use what they see will be persuasive arguments and expect to achieve their goal even if they have to make up a story at times. It is entirely possible that their arguments are flawlessly supported with proper data and information, but the Japanese will become skeptical of such arguments. In Japan, having a reputation for being *rikutsu-poi* or "overly logical" negatively affects the negotiator's reputation for integrity and trustworthiness because the Japanese are averse to aggressive logical attacks. Throughout their socialization from early childhood, they have been taught to hold back what they really want to say for the sake of maintaining interpersonal harmony. The pseudo-logical arguments or "arguments for argument's sake" sometimes used by Americans will not work with the Japanese.

Coping with Frustrations at the Negotiation Table

At the stage of exchanging task-related information, many problems emerge from the contrasting negotiation styles of Westerners and Japanese. Because these problems are caused by differences in business practices and social customs, it is not easy to cope with them without exercising cultural empathy and mental flexibility. Westerners frequently complain that the Japanese are slower and more deliberate and that it takes them a long time to make concessions. Westerners also complain that the Japanese retreat into vague statements or silence when complications develop and make frequent referrals to superiors or the head office. They also find some of the Japanese nonverbal behaviors to be complex and confusing.

The most serious problem that busy Western negotiators must cope with is a much slower style of bargaining in Japan. It does not mean that Japanese negotiators are not conscious of time and deadlines, but they want to be cautious and thorough. Unlike Western negotiators, they are not used to making a deal or signing a contract with a lot of contingencies. If they find any unclear or doubtful points, they will ask the opponents to restate and clarify them again and again until they are fully satisfied. They will also take a team approach and always try to reach a consensus among themselves before responding to anything. If they are pressured to make a quick decision, they will become skeptical of the opponents' intention and act even more slowly. It is also important to recognize that the Japanese are more likely to make concessions toward the end of negotiation instead of taking the sequential and logical approach preferred by the Western negotiators. Obviously, the Westerners must not rush the Japanese to accept their way of making concessions, even though the negotiation might not be progressing as quickly as they wish.

Another major problem for Western negotiators is that Japanese negotiators will make vague statements, pause frequently, and stop talking when they run into difficulties. In contrast, Americans generally become more aggressive and argumentative and try to persuade the Japanese side with threats, promises, and logical reasoning. Such aggressive tactics will backfire; they will cause the Japanese side to show even more patience and perseverance and more indifference to time pressures. This Japanese behavior is a show of both defiance and anxiety. The only solution for this problem is to create a pleasant and amicable atmosphere by reducing all social tensions coming from the ongoing bargaining. It is always a good idea to take a long coffee break to engage in social conversation or to reschedule subsequent negotiation sessions on another day. Once social tensions emerge from open conflicts over difficult issues, it will be impossible to proceed until the amicable atmosphere is rekindled. Having a nice dinner or taking a day off from negotiations to play a round of golf will definitely help reduce the social tensions. The Japanese feel more comfortable making negative statements in informal situations. Sometimes, they even reveal their "true mind" smilingly and half-jokingly under the pretense of being a little drunk. This does not mean that they are dishonest or cunning; they are simply trying to save face for both sides.

Still another cause of frustration can be that Japanese negotiating team members usually have little or no authority to make on-the-spot decisions. There are several reasons why they need to confer with superiors at the home office. In Japan, all major business decisions are made through *ringi* or "group decision making." Further, Japanese negotiators are not usually given authority to make even minor concessions that have not been approved prior to negotiation. They abhor taking personal risks to expedite the decision-making process, even if they themselves believe in the merit of doing so. They are extremely cautious and worried about disrupting interpersonal harmony by taking the credit for "selfish" personal achievement. In fact, even the chief Japanese negotiator will hesitate to make decisions on his own,

103

unless he happens to be the founder and the majority shareholder of the company he represents. The most frustrating experience for Western negotiators is for the Japanese side to say, "By the way, we'll need to call Tokyo just to make sure," when the Westerners thought that they could finally close the deal after hard bargaining. If Western negotiators wish to avoid this last-minute surprise, they should not push the Japanese opponents too hard to squeeze out a positive answer. This "positive answer" can only be "Japanese yes," which really means, "I say 'yes' for now because you force me to, but I still have to check with the home office." It is wise to follow an old Japanese saying, *isogaba maware,* or "If you are in a hurry, take a longer way." It is also necessary to know who the real decision makers are and not to assume that the Japanese representatives have enough authority and responsibility to consummate a deal. Westerners must realize that they are negotiating not only with the Japanese negotiators sitting across the table, but also with their colleagues and superiors in Japan.

Japanese nonverbal behaviors at the negotiation table can be puzzling to Westerners. March claims that for the Japanese, nonverbal expressions are strategies for concealing, for avoiding communication, and for becoming invisible. "The Japanese are exceptionally skillful at nondisclosure, at masking and restraint of emotions; they are indeed hard to read, especially for the inexperienced Westerner. . . . Nondisclosure is deeply ingrained in Japanese culture. . . . Learning to put a 'face' over one's true feelings and emotions is part of growing up for every Japanese."[18]

Some of the most puzzling of Japanese nonverbal behaviors are unique Japanese facial expressions, gestures, and postures. The Japanese are trained to put on an impassive or stoical face in formal situations. They almost never smile at strangers, and they usually look away when they have accidental eye contact with one another. This is *shirankao* or "knowing-nothing face," which is used when they wish to avoid personal involvement. For example, during a contract negotiation when open confrontation becomes unbearably tense, the Japanese may use *shirankao* and totally ignore what the opponents are trying to do. In response to aggressive persuasion, they may give "yes" answers that do not mean "yes" or just keep on nodding with meaningless grunts.

Interpretation of Japanese eye contact is another problem. In Western culture, sustained direct eye contact usually indicates that people are interested, honest, and positive. In Japanese culture, however, sustained direct eye contact means aggression, rudeness, insistence on equality, and even belligerence. Consequently, Japanese negotiators frequently close or shift their eyes during negotiation. This Japanese behavior is frustrating for Westerners because they rely upon having good eye contact for direct feedback. Lack of direct eye contact makes it difficult for them to determine whether or not they have been successful in persuading their Japanese opponents. On rare occasions when the Japanese want to show anger or displeasure, they use a steely, hostile stare to express their feelings. They sometimes use *nusumi mi* or "snatching look" at the eyes of the opposing negotiators. Instead of engaging in direct eye contact, they also use *yokome* or "looking out of the corner of the eyes." Undoubtedly, attaching meanings to various forms of Japanese eye contact based on Western interpretations will cause misunderstandings.

The Japanese use their mouths rather expressively in nonverbal communication. Opening the mouth wide while listening is to be avoided in Japanese social etiquette. Not only it is impolite, but it also suggests stupidity, boredom, or lack of mental alertness; the Japanese usually close their mouths firmly in formal situations. To express bewilderment, anxiety, or difficulty, they may form the mouth into an "O." They may literally drop their jaws when they hear something really unbelievable. When they are very upset, they will close their mouths very tightly and stare at the people who have offended them. Young Japanese women often cover their mouths with their hands to hide immoderate laughter or giggling.

Japanese smiles and laughter carry more than universal meanings of happiness, joy, or agreement. A few forms of Japanese smiles and laughter convey entirely different meanings. One example is the smile of embarrassment, which means, "I'm sorry, I made a mistake. I smiled because I wanted to hide my embarrassment." Another example is the laughter of contempt, which means, "You must be kidding. You cannot possibly make such a stupid demand!" A Japanese negotiator might "half-jokingly" or "laughingly" protest the unreasonable demand in order not to squarely confront and offend the guilty party, but he is dead serious and really upset. Another puzzling Japanese smile is the *tsukuri warai* or "made-up smile," which means, "I am smiling because I don't want to dampen the pleasant atmosphere of this negotiation. You shouldn't think that I am agreeing with you."

Certain Japanese gestures and postures can also puzzle the uninformed Westerner. The hand gesture meaning "me" is pointing to one's nose with the index finger. "No, I don't agree with you" or "That's no good" is shown by moving the open right palm sideways as if fanning. Japanese men clasp their hands tightly, place them on the table, and lean forward when they are serious. They put both elbows on the table and support their chin *(hohozue)* when they are bored or tired. They cross their arms in front of the body, lean backward, and close their eyes when they have to listen to a long presentation. Westerners need to recogize that these non-verbal behaviors do not mean that they are totally inattentive or sleeping. In fact, they are probably concentrating on what is being presented.

Finally, side-talk in Japanese among Japanese negotiators can be very annoying to their Western counterparts. When the Western negotiators encounter this situation, they show annoyance either by negative facial expressions or by fidgeting. They may even interrupt the side-talk by saying, "Excuse me, could you speak in English? We don't understand what you are saying." No matter how annoying it may be, it is absolutely unwise to interrupt the Japanese negotiators' side-talk and ask for interpretation of what they have been talking about. Instead, if the Japanese team members talk among themselves too many times, it is a good idea to suggest a recess and ask them to come back as soon as they can reach a consensus among themselves.

The training video made by Intercultural Training Resources explains that frequent side-talk can be a sign of good progress in negotiation. It also explains, "Japanese are not only concerned that they do not misrepresent the feeling of the 'group' to which they belong, but they also must pay special heed to the rank and hierarchy of the context in which they find themselves. For these reasons it is frequently necessary to confer with other team members before speaking, to be sure that what one says has the full support of colleagues and superiors."[19]

After the Negotiation

Once verbal agreements have been reached, it is time to start working on a written contract. In the Western business context, the exact wording of terms and conditions is of absolute importance. In the Japanese business context, establishing solid interpersonal relationships with each member of the opposing negotiation team is considered much more important. Japanese businessmen do not like to sign a lengthy American-style contract with carefully worded clauses regarding all circumstances, contingencies, and specific legal actions to be taken in case of breach of the contract. This particular Japanese attitude does not mean that the Japanese ignore contracts; they just have a different approach to the implementation of written contracts.

It is a commonly accepted practice in Japan to begin production or start selling before the final contract is signed if both parties feel that they have reached verbal understandings. It is also true that many Japanese sign contracts without having their lawyers review them. They do so because they believe in the doctrine of *jijō henkō* or "changed circumstances."[20] Most Japanese businessmen assume that rights and duties under the contract, even when written down, are provisional or tentative rather than absolute. They believe that the specific items of a contract are always open to renegotiation whenever economic circumstances change drastically. They ask for revisions or modifications of a contract not based on the terms of that particular contract but on the "strong friendship" established during the negotiation. They also insist on compromises by promising *nagai tsukiai* or "a long-term relationship." Their premise is that both parties to a contract should help each other during an economic downturn. They may say, "You must help us now when we are in a serious trouble. We'll be sure to return your favor during our long-term relationship." However, some dishonest Japanese businessmen use this promise of *nagai tsukiai* as a "trick" or bait to gain an unfair advantage over the other party, having no intention of standing behind it.

If Western businesspeople want to avoid contractual disputes with their Japanese counterparts, it is absolutely necessary to have a contract in both English and Japanese written by bilingual attorneys who are familiar with both Western and Japanese business laws. Their attorneys must make sure that every important clause is explained to and understood fully by the Japanese side. It is usually necessary to have a professional translator translate the original English language contract into Japanese as reference. In case of a contractual dispute, the English contract takes precedence over the Japanese translation of the original contract.

Signing Ceremonies

The Japanese love ceremonies and celebrations. Just like the signing of a major treaty between two nations, Japanese companies hold a formal signing ceremony when sealing a major business deal. American firms may consider it a waste of time and money, but the signing ceremony plays a number of important cultural functions in Japan. The ceremony allows the top executives of both sides to meet and sign the contract. This signing is not only the official approval of the contract, but also serves as public notice of the action. The participants of a typical Japanese signing ceremony include the chairman of the board, the president, senior vice presidents, vice presidents, division managers, section chiefs, and junior staff members of the company. In addition, *raihin* or "guests of honor" are invited to participate. They may include bank managers, executives of suppliers, local politicians, advertising agency managers, officials of trade associations, and TV and newspaper reporters. Sometimes, the trade attaché of the foreign embassy of the foreign partner's country is invited to witness the celebration.

At the signing ceremony, top executives of both companies give formal congratulation speeches before the actual signing. Immediately afterward, gifts are exchanged to commemorate the occasion. The gift does not have to be an expensive one, but it should match the size or the importance of the contract entered into. For example, the American side may give an oil painting of New York skyscrapers and the Japanese side may reciprocate with a samurai helmet replica in a glass case.

The signing ceremony is usually followed by an elaborate cocktail reception where all the participants can mingle and socialize. At the reception, news reporters will interview the executives. Many Japanese companies hold a special golf tournament after the signing ceremony for more socializing, and commemorative golf trophies and prizes are given to all participants. It is common practice to take many pictures of the important executives and the honored guests at the ceremony, the cocktail party, and during the golf tournament. These photographs are put into a nice photo album and sent to the important participants with a formal letter of appreciation. This personal touch will work wonders when the contract is implemented. Now that all participants are remembered by their names and faces, they will be able to establish better per-son-to-person relationships.

Follow-up Communications for Personal Relationships

Once the contract is signed, Western businessmen tend to put it aside and forget to nurture the personal relationships. This is a big mistake, because Japanese businessmen always want to stay in constant personal contact with their business associates. They will not just pick up a telephone or send a facsimile message to send greetings. Instead, they prefer to make personal visits as frequently as possible in order to get acquainted again with the individuals in charge and to informally obtain feedback regarding the ongoing business. Most Japanese companies doing business with foreign companies make it a practice to make *hyōkei hōmon* or a "courtesy visit" to the headquarters of the foreign partners. Even if it is to be only an annual courtesy visit without any particular business purpose, they believe that nurturing the personal relationship is crucial to continuing a successful business relationship. Some Japanese companies sponsor an annual golf tournament and invite the foreign partners to participate. Other companies may host the golf tournament on alternate years in Japan and ask the foreign partners to reciprocate in their home country. During these golf tournaments, the executives from both sides will renew friendships and talk about problems of doing business together under the pretense of socializing on the golf course. The Japanese executives may non-chalantly make requests or suggestions on certain pending issues, hoping that their foreign counterparts will take them up and look into them when they return to their offices.

Although it may not be necessary for foreign companies to adhere to the traditional Japanese custom of gift giving, it is important to remember that all Japanese companies give out *ochūgen* (midsummer gifts) and *oseibo* (year-end gifts.) These gifts are tokens of gratitude to client companies or individuals that have given them lots of business or favors. The gifts are also used to make the recipients feel obligated to continue the ongoing business relationships. Nowadays many Japanese have adopted the Western custom of sending Christmas cards to foreign business partners. Gift giving and sending Christmas cards are important prerequisites for continuing successful business relations with the Japanese.

One other important consideration is not to switch the executives or the managers who have been in charge of doing business with Japan. Ideally, the same executives and staff members who negotiated the original contract should continue to deal with their Japanese counterparts. If they are transferred to another department, they should be included in future meetings as observers or advisors. If this is inconvenient for some reason, it is a good idea to invite them to the social events given in honor of the visiting Japanese associates. The Japanese negotiation team members will be disappointed if they cannot maintain personal relationships with their "old friends." They find it difficult to start a new business relationship all over again with "strangers." They also want to continue relying on those foreign counterparts who remember *kuchiyakusoku* or "unwritten verbal understandings" obtained during the original negotiation sessions.

Conflict Resolution

In the Western business context, contractual disputes are almost always handled by attorneys and settled in court. Businesses file suits and countersuits to settle the disputes, even though they might have had years of friendly and cooperative business relationships. In contrast, Japanese businesses prefer to settle their disputes through mutual consultation *(hanashiai)*, mediation *(chūkai)* or arbitration *(chūsai)* without going to court. They rarely sue each other because their business relationships have always been personal and subjective in nature. The Japanese generally find litigation distasteful and destructive, and they even feel ashamed to have created such a situation in the first place. They would rather compromise and settle every dispute out of court to avoid the public embarrassment and bad publicity of a long legal battle. This avoidance behavior is rooted in the all-inclusive clause written in all Japanese contracts, "All items not found in this contract will be deliberated and decided upon in a spirit of honesty and trust."

For both legal and cultural reasons, litigation by Western businesspeople will usually end up in a miserable failure. Japan's legal system is based on civil law, rather than on the common law tradition of Britain and the United States. Japan has only 14,433 lawyers (one for every 8,567 Japanese citizens) compared to more than 700,000 in the United States (one for every 356 Americans). For the most part, these Japanese lawyers are trained specialists in criminal defense and civil litigation. Japan's legal system prohibits unlicensed foreign lawyers from engaging in legal practice and also prohibits them from forming partnerships with Japanese lawyers. Even America's powerful and globally networked international law firms ran into adamant opposition from the small but growing number of Japanese lawyers who specialize in international corporate law. Cultural reasons for shunning American law firms' activities include fears that Japan's nonlitigious society will be corrupted by combative American "overlawyering," reluctance of Japanese lawyers to file lawsuits on speculation because Japan's courts offer little opportunity for legal maneuvering and the belief of Japanese lawyers that their mission is to protect fundamental human rights and realize social justice instead of protecting business interests.[21] In this context, litigation is obviously not the best solution for contractual disputes.

Mutual Consultation

The very first step of resolving any and all business disputes in Japan is to engage in mutual consultation. Instead of immediately hiring legal counsel, those individuals who negotiated the original contract will call an informal meeting to discuss the problems. This *hanashiai* can be easily arranged because they usually keep up their friendly personal relationships beyond the business relationship.

However, the initial discussion of disputes should be conducted at *jimu reberu* (staff members' level) without any executives present. This is an important means of saving face for the executives who approved the original agreement, which may have to be adjusted or renegotiated. Only after the staff members have come up with a few mutually acceptable solutions will they consult the top executives for advice and endorsement of the best alternative.

It would be impolite and also ineffective to pin down the top Japanese executives who appear to be in charge and talk to them directly. Important decisions will require group consensus in Japanese companies.*

Mediation

If informal mutual consultations do not work, a mediator *(chūkaisha)* will be asked to help resolve the dispute. The mediator can be the introducer, an attorney, an influential politician, a senior banker, an executive director of a trade association, or an international business consultant. He must be known as a neutral and fair-minded person who can easily establish interpersonal relations, who is considered highly trustworthy, reliable, and knowledgeable, and who has many years of experience in international business. Ideally, he also should be a bilingual and bicultural person. He will find it difficult to mediate an international dispute if he has to rely on an interpreter.

An effective mediator must be able to manage the mediating process properly. He should know when face-to-face contact between the parties to a conflict is preferable and when it is to be avoided. Early in the mediation process, it is useful for him to call a joint meeting with both parties to make accurate assessment of their level of disagreement and of their actual positions. He can observe how receptive the parties are to each other and determine whether or not further face-to-face meetings can facilitate better understanding between them. He also needs to conduct private sessions with each party separately to understand their respective positions. Just listening to each of the bitterly contesting parties gives them a chance to openly vent their hostilities. In this way, the mediator functions as a tension reliever.

Once hostilities are out in the open, the mediator helps each party overcome or modify the negative feelings in order to resolve the conflict. Then, he conveys information very selectively after careful evaluation of every pertinent fact. He must pick key

---

* See chapter 6 for detailed discussion on group decision making.

phrases, ideas, and concepts and present them to both sides. Suggestions and recommendations should be presented tentatively rather than absolutely, and overstatements should be avoided. At this stage, the bilingual ability of a mediator plays a very critical role. For example, a statement by the American side such as "We have several problems that we need to address immediately" may cause serious trouble if it is translated directly into Japanese word for word. In the Japanese language, there is only one word, *mondai,* for both "problem" and "trouble." The mediator must know whether *mondai* is to be used to imply "problem" or "trouble." The word "immediately" cannot be translated literally into Japanese and conveyed to the Japanese side because the meaning of "urgency of action" is colored by the relative status relationship between the two parties. If the Japanese side is the buyer, the mediator cannot rush them to take immediate action. He must be very sensitive to language usage and to the specific situation.

Control of detrimental rumors is especially critical in multinational settings. Negative rumors can be one of the most serious obstacles to conflict resolution. Because most rumors are exaggerations or distortions of facts, groundless accusations, careless statements, or personal opinions, they often create unwarranted fears and distrust in the minds of those involved in the conflict. Although an experienced mediator sometimes uses rumors to his advantage, such use can be risky. Most often the mediator needs to closely monitor and stop all detrimental rumors immediately. He should take countermeasures to dispel any rumors by flooding the communication channels with credible counterevidence and by discrediting the disrupting parties as irresponsible and unreliable. In certain situations, he can counter detrimental rumors by openly discussing them with both parties.

A good mediator constantly encourages the opposing parties to reevaluate and modify their positions. He will probe the positions with them, searching for points of potential compromise. He often plays devil's advocate to stimulate internal inquiries and discussion of alternative solutions, showing both parties a number of different options for a solution. He also tries to find allies among members of each party who are inclined to adopt middle-ground positions. Then he encourages those allies to become supporters who, in turn, convince others to accept his recommendations. For example, he will find one or two top Japanese executives who seem to be more friendly and sympathetic toward the problem at hand and diplomatically entice them to act as his inside supporters.

The mediator needs to convince the individuals involved that they can shift their positions without losing face. This is an extremely important consideration when mediating a dispute with the Japanese, because they are always very conscious of face-saving. In addition, he must persuade both parties that they will have to give up some points to reach a mutually acceptable settlement. Finally, he must convince both parties that the final settlement that he mediated is the best solution under the circumstances.

Arbitration

Arbitration is another form of conflict resolution that involves a third party. Arbitration grants the third party the power to study the conflict and reach a settlement. There are two types of arbitration: binding and nonbinding. Binding arbitration requires that both parties agree to be bound by the settlement worked out by an arbitrator, whereas the nonbinding arbitration allows either party to reject the settlement.

There are three important assumptions regarding arbitration:

1. Clear procedural standards will have been worked out and agreed upon in advance by both sides.

2. Judgment will be made based on the facts of the case after each side has presented all materials relevant to the case.

3. The parties involved will accept the decision of the arbitrator. [22]

Arbitration of an international dispute often creates unique problems. In the first place, an arbitrator in one country may not be able to render a truly rational and completely fair decision for the party from the other country. For instance, a Japanese judge may be prejudiced against the foreign company and may favor the Japanese company. It is also true that procedures and rules of conduct may differ. Therefore, all contracts between companies from two different countries should include an arbitration clause that delineates specific legal procedures and actions, jurisdiction, payment of fees and expenses, and the country in which arbitration takes place.

In Japan, the Japanese Commercial Arbitration Association (JCAA) conducts hearings on disputes, but getting satisfactory arbitration is time consuming and difficult. The JCAA acts more like a mediator and tries to induce out-of-court settlements from both parties. It is reported that only 1 percent of all cases brought to the JCAA results in binding arbitration. Arbitration is not a well established and acceptable means for Japanese business enterprises as yet.

Foreign businesspeople may wish to see the Japanese legal system operate like the Western legal system, but it is dangerous to assume that Western legal codes and practices will be applied in solving international business disputes in Japan. The Japanese government also promotes the use of a less disruptive means when it comes to settling international disputes. Although it may be possible to hire American lawyers in Tokyo who specialize in the legal aspects of international business, they cannot function as efficiently and effectively in Japan as they can in their own country. Therefore, the best advice to foreign businesspeople is to avoid filing lawsuits; under current circumstances, the Japanese approach of seeking a resolution through cooperation and compromises seems the only prudent way of solving contractual problems with the Japanese.

Decision Making in Japanese Business Organizations

The process of *ringi* or group decision making in Japanese business organizations has always been a popular subject of academic investigation. *Ringi* is considered uniquely Japanese because it is so different from the common practices of decision making in Western business organizations. Another Japanese method of decision making considered peculiar by Westerners is *kaigi* or "meeting." Although *kaigi* appears similar to the business meeting conducted in Western business organizations, it is conducted quite differently. Many Western scholars and businesspeople are very critical of Japanese decision-making processes as intuitive and irrational.

Glazer says,

> In business situations, the Japanese are unable to act analytically. To them, a subjective interpretation of problems is considerably more important than economic considerations. Their approach is intuitive, as opposed to American businessmen's approach, which is based on reasoning, propositions, and logical inferences from objective data. In Japan, decisions are made not on the basis of facts but on the basis of moods, because the Japanese are primarily concerned with harmoniously working out problems without causing interpersonal frictions.[1]

Bairy explains,

> Americans are accustomed to seeing a line of authority in a business with final accountability concentrated

in one man who is perceived as "outstanding," but in Japan, authority is delegated to one who "stands in" rather than "out." A Japanese will not run the risk of taking over the responsibility and making independent decisions. The function of a Japanese leader is that of a "mediator" or of a "harmonizing agent." Since the responsibility does not rest on any one person, but in the group, there is no delegation or line of authority. Distribution of authority and responsibility is also made according to the seniority and chronological age of executives. Therefore, senior members tend to assume more important roles and positions, although they may not necessarily be the most capable members. The notion of "decision by a majority" does not exist in the traditional Japanese process of decision-making or *ringi-seido,* because every member concerned must approve the proposal; it must be a unanimous decision. There is no decision, in the American sense, which is obtained through reasoning. The word "decision" should be replaced by "confirmation," as this process is confirmation of something which has already been approved informally by every member of the organization.[2]

Adams also explains, "Perhaps no other single factor in Japanese government and business seems quite so incomprehensible to the Westerner, whose whole life conditions him to the making of quick decisions, for which he then assumes responsibility." He also quotes the report of Captain Ellis Zacharias of the United States wartime Naval Intelligence, who says, "No Japanese, regardless of rank and position, is so constituted that as an individual, is willing or able to assume responsibility for important decisions without the benefit of lengthy and repeated discussions sufficient to convince him that he does not carry the responsibility alone."[3]

De Mente aptly describes the Japanese style of *kaigi* as "talking things to death." He says, "One of the Japanese customs that foreigners often find frustrating, and sometimes regard as a malicious ploy to gain an advantage, is their practice of holding what Westerners regards as excessive numbers of meetings to discuss business or other propositions, and to generally drag out discussions over inordinately long periods of time."[4]

The above criticisms by Western scholars are not based on totally inaccurate observations of Japanese businessmen's behavior, but they do reflect a judgment of the Japanese from their own culture-bound criteria of rationality and efficiency. Their criticisms could also be based on their naive assumption that the ways of thinking or the nature of interpersonal relationships among Japanese businessmen will change or become totally Westernized as the result of the rapid economic and industrial growth patterned after the industrialized nations. Westerners must recognize that this seemingly absurd and irrational decision-making behavior of the Japanese can be legitimate and rational in the Japanese cultural context.

Noda claims that "Japanese uniqueness" has been exaggerated by Western scholars because of the confusion between formal and informal practices. In fact, Japanese enterprises, like enterprises in other advanced countries in the free-world economy, must give priority to economic rationality if they hope to realize profits. During its thousands of years of historical development in isolation, Japan has developed a society that is decidedly more homogeneous than most other countries. This homogeneity in race, language, culture, and lifestyle facilitates establishment of informal ties among individuals. In organizations where individuals work together continuously for a long time, informal custom has far more power than the formal system in regulating the daily activities of the system's members.[5] Therefore, it is important to examine the nature and functions of Japanese society that have created and perpetuated the particular type of interpersonal relationships and decision-making practices in Japanese business organizations.

Decision Makers in the Japanese Business Organization

Unlike their Western counterparts, Japanese executives and managers are not independent decision makers. Despite the fact that they may hold comparable job titles of top executives, managers, and supervisors found in a Western business organization, they neither exercise the same authority nor take on the same responsibility. There are eleven managerial ranks within a Japanese organization: chairman *(kaichō)*, president *(shachō)*, vice president *(fuku shachō)*, senior executive managing director *(senmu torishimariyaku)*, executive managing director *(jōmu torishimariyaku)*, director *(torishimariyaku)*, general manager *(buchō)*, deputy general manager *(buchō dairi)*, section chief *(kachō)*, deputy section chief *(kachō dairi)*, and supervisor *(kakarichō)*.

In Japan, the chairman's function is not identical to that of the chairman of the board or the chief executive officer in Western countries. The chairman has held the position of president for several years before taking this position.* The important difference is that he is no longer the decision maker as he has relinquished all authority and decision-making power to his successor, the president *(shachō)*. He now has an honorary position for a few years before retirement and is expected to play an advisory role only.

The president's official title in Japanese is *daihyō torishimariyaku shachō* (president and representative director). He is the highest-ranking executive and has the authority given by the Board of Directors *(Torishimariyaku kai)* to legally represent the company.

The senior managing director *(senmu torishimariyaku)* is second in command and has more power and authority than other lower-ranked directors. He is assigned to coordinate the entire operations of the company and reports directly to the president. He officially represents the company during the president's absence. The executive managing director *(jōmu torishimariyaku)* is the top executive of a division within the company and also reports to the president. All of the above executives are the regular members of *Torishimariyaku kai,* the legal decision-making body defined by the Japanese Commercial Law. The title of director *(torishimariyaku)* also applies to a low-ranked director who could also be the general manager *(buchō)*.†

The general manager is responsible for overseeing day-to-day operations of his division and is assisted by his deputy general

---

* Promotion to the position is similar to "being kicked upstairs" or semi-retirement. It is customary that the chairman continue to serve as part-time *sōdanyaku* (advisor) for an additional year or two years before full retirement.

† A low-ranked director without authority or power to make crucial decisions is called *hiratori* or a person with the title of director but without executive privileges.

manager *(buchō dairi)*. The section chief *(kachō)* is in charge of his section, the first-level management unit, and works under the general manager. He is assisted by the deputy section chief *(kachō dairi)* and the supervisor *(kakarichō)*. The section chief is the busiest person in the organization sandwiched between the general manager and his immediate subordinates.

Unlike in Western businesses, the members of the Board of Directors in most Japanese big businesses are not outside directors. Instead, they are insiders who have achieved their positions within the company hierarchy, and they concurrently hold regular working positions. Even auditors are not external directors, but are chosen from among senior directors within the higher executive ranks. All executives are continually mindful of their relative status in a complex hierarchy of interpersonal relationships that has been established over many years of working together. Many executives and managers who have achieved the same rank are hesitant to act as equals. Previous *sempai-kōhai* (senior-junior) relationships can never be forgotten. Even when executive positions are reversed, newly appointed executives are expected to treat their seniors (in age and seniority) with respect and deference.

The Board of Directors of a Japanese company is not exactly a voting body in a Western sense because decisions are hardly ever made by majority rule. Likewise, a Japanese company president will not make major decisions on his own unless he can obtain a complete consensus through the process of *ringi*. In rare instances when the president is the founder or owner of the company, he may use *tsuru no hitokoe* (one screech of the crane) or a proclamation of his own decision. In some other instances, *ato-ringi* (after-the-fact consensus) is used to expedite decision making. For example, the owner-president of a family-owned company may make a decision based on intuition from his years of business experience. Then he will ask his subordinates to write up a *ringi* proposal and have them justify the action that he has taken on his own initiative. In such a case, *ringi* is sought as a formality to authorize the decision previously reached. In a nutshell, decisions in Japanese business organizations are based on some form of a consensus before or after the actions are taken. From the Japanese point of view, majority rule decision making often destroys the solidarity of the group. Obtaining agreement from everyone is still the most widespread form of traditional decision making in Japan under almost all circumstances.

This unanimity, however, does not necessarily mean that a decision was reached after thorough debate and formulation by all the members of the management. In some cases a decision was pushed along by one or two people with great initiative, and the remainder of the members expressed consent later. In other cases, the final decision maker proposes a plan that all members agree to follow after having expressed a variety of differing opinions.

It is commonly assumed that decision making by consensus in Japan means no one individual will take responsibility for a decision because the responsibility is divided among all members. However, getting a consensus is separate from attributing responsibility for success or failure. Even in cases when a decision is made by all members, if the result is a serious failure, the company president, either alone or with a small group of senior directors, will take responsibility for the failure. In other cases, a junior director who has had no actual influence in a final decision may be forced to resign. Of course, it is quite common for responsibility to be shouldered by the person(s) responsible for advancing a given decision.[6] A severe punishment commonly used against an executive or a manager responsible for a major mistake is *sasen* (demotion plus transfer) or *shima nagashi* (exile to a remote island). The guilty party will suddenly be transferred to a miserable position at a pathetic branch office within Japan or in a foreign country.

Ringi or Group Decision Making

Ringi literally means "circulate a proposal, discuss, and decide." This is still the most common process of decision-making in Japan, although some innovative decision-making processes are being introduced through computerization of office procedures. *Ringi* process begins with *kiansha* (plan initiator), usually a lower or middle-ranking manager (supervisor or section chief), who is put in charge of drafting a *ringisho* (proposal). Before drafting this document, he discusses the general idea informally with key executives, managers, and supervisors. Only after getting fairly positive initial reactions from them will he draft the proposal document, which includes the request for a decision, supporting data and information, detailed explanations, and justifications. This informal discussion is called *nemawashi*, which literally means "twisting the tree roots around." In practice, *nemawashi* refers to holding many face-to-face informal, behind-the-scene discussions about a proposal among all the people who would be concerned with or involved in implementing any decision to be made later. In other words, the proposal is turned around and around, viewed and deliberated from every angle, before it is brought out into the open as an official or formal proposal. The act of *nemawashi* is analogous to twisting a planted tree around to cut off bothersome roots or "objections" so that it can be uprooted easily. *Nemawashi* then is a sounding board for unofficially testing the responses to an idea without exposing or endangering anyone before making a commitment. It is a lobbying mechanism used by any individual or group wanting to get a project through the system.[7]

Once a *ringi* proposal is completed, the initiator will circulate it to every executive and manager, who will be asked to approve it after careful review. The circulation is executed in reverse order of each individual's hierarchical position, beginning with the lowest-ranked supervisor, to middle management, top management, and finally to the president. The cover sheet of the proposal has many small boxes for *han* (seal of approval) to be affixed by all those who will review and approve it. The proper order of circulation is strictly adhered to because skipping any person on the hierarchical ladder will cause serious procedural and interpersonal problems. If any of the managers or executives have questions or objections, the initiator will have to answer them in person. If he cannot win everyone's approval, the proposal will be held back for a long time and will not reach the president's desk. The decision can be delayed indefinitely until the person who is objecting receives convincing justification based on new data and information. If the initiator cannot overcome the objections by himself, he will have to ask his immediate superior or someone who is influential in top management to help him. When all the seals of approval are obtained successfully, the document will be hand-delivered to the president for his approval. This final approval from the president, called *kessai*, is the last step in the *ringi* decision-making process.

Suppose that a Japanese manufacturer has decided to build an electronic component factory in Hawai'i. A section chief will be asked by his superiors to begin a *ringi* process. He becomes the plan initiator, who in turn assigns to his subordinates the task of gathering pertinent information and necessary data to write up a *ringi* proposal. As the preparation of this document progresses, he will have informal *nemawashi* meetings with those who are directly or indirectly involved in the project. During this process, he tries to find exactly who will be supporting or objecting to this project. For example, the marketing department head is supporting it because he believes that an increased local production of electronic components will mean a much larger market share in the United States and elimination of the worries over import quotas and taxes. The production manager is vehemently objecting to any attempt to transfer productions overseas, as he is afraid of the hollowing of the company's manufacturing sector and the loss of employment among skilled factory workers. He is also worried about the quality of workers in Hawai'i, because almost all assembly-line workers will be former pineapple farm workers. The vice president of finance is hesitant about investing a huge sum of money in any new project at this time because Japan's economy has been sluggish for the past several years. The initiator's task is to overcome these objections. He must collect reliable information to persuade the objecting parties that anticipated negative effects of overseas production are not real problems. He must also convince the vice president that this is the best time to invest in Hawai'i by pointing out that the State of Hawaii will provide tax incentives and special funds for training new factory workers.

If he cannot win full support of the production manager and the vice president, he will have to solicit other supportive executives or managers to act as allies. He may ask the personnel manager, his good friend, to assist him in persuading the production manager instead of arguing or confronting him face to face. He could perhaps contact the head of the finance division, who happens to be a graduate of the same university and a weekend golf partner, and beg him to help persuade the vice president on the merits of investing at this opportune time.

In the Japanese business organization, *kashi-kari kankei* (give-and-take relationship) among its members is a very important social asset, and it gives power and authority to an individual who can accumulate favors.[8] In this case, the personnel manager and the head of the finance division can ask favors of the production manager and the vice president of finance because they have already established an all-important *kashi-kari kankei* through exchanging many personal favors in the past.

Although there will be formal presentations at a conference table or in individual offices, the initiator will have conducted most of the *nemawashi* over drinks, dinners, or golf games. It is absolutely necessary for him to secure a firm commitment from each and every individual executive and manager in this manner before proceeding. Otherwise, his efforts will never result in unanimous approval of his *ringi* proposal. It is indeed an illogical and inefficient decision-making process compared to a more logical and confrontational Western style of decision making, but *ringi* is culturally appropriate and the most suitable method of decision making in the context of Japanese corporate culture.

125

Kaigi or Business Meeting

Kaigi in Japanese business organizations appears on the surface to be similar to a business meeting or conference in Western business organizations. However, it differs from a typical Western-style meeting in its purpose and procedure, the participation of those attending, and the content of what is brought up for open discussion.

Generally speaking, the purpose of a Western-style business meeting is to facilitate decision making in face-to-face situations. In contrast, the Japanese meeting is an occasion to formally confirm what has been already decided informally through intensive *nemawashi*. In many instances, Japanese participants go through the ritual of asking questions and debating certain points, but they are merely saying what has been discussed and agreed upon to obtain *shōdaku* (approval) from all other participants. This type of meeting seems to work in Japanese business organizations because of the widespread use of *nemawashi*. In the Western cultural context, it is not considered a betrayal to change one's mind during the discussion about what has been informally agreed on prior to the meeting if a much better idea or new compelling evidence is presented. In the Japanese cultural context, however, such changing of one's mind is a serious social infraction and betrayal of interpersonal trust because any agreement reached during informal consultations is considered a firm commitment. The commitments made during *nemawashi* are not tentative commitments or personal opinions that Western businesspeople usually try to obtain when going through the process of "touching the bases."

The leadership role of a Japanese chairperson is different from that of his Western counterpart. The chairperson's main role is not to aggressively take direct control over the decision-making process, but to mediate the consensus-building process among all participants. In fact, his assistant, who is the second-ranking person, does most of the talking and directing other participants to contribute to the ongoing discussion in a predetermined order. Each participant usually presents a brief report prepared in advance and asks for everyone's approval. In rare instances, he may encounter strong objections, but he usually receives only a few questions for clarification. He has probably talked to every participant about his report and obtained informal concurrence before the meeting. There will not be open discussion of issues, uninhibited expression of diverse opinions, or serious evaluation of alternative solutions.

If someone, especially a junior participant, wishes to voice his opinion, he will preface his remarks by saying, "I may be making a judgment based on my limited knowledge on this subject, but . . . " or "Please correct me if you think I am wrong, but . . . " Because he is extremely concerned about causing loss of face or disrupting interpersonal harmony by making "foolish statements," he needs to take a tentative approach and also show humility. Other participants are also hesitant to voice frank opinions or disagreements, because even constructive criticisms on specific points are often taken as personal attacks or insults. All participants tend to look for subtle verbal or nonverbal cues and try to understand how the other participants feel about what is being discussed.

In contrast, an American chairperson guides, stimulates, and controls the discussion. He makes certain that the agenda is followed, and he encourages each participant to voice different opinions and observations without hesitation. When it is necessary, he will volunteer to explain, clarify, or make internal summaries of what has been discussed. As he is accustomed to using a "top-down" approach, he is in total control and retains his decision-making power. Other participants are independent thinkers and are willing to voice strong opinions and even objections—at least in their own areas of specialization—without fear of reprisal.

The behavior of Japanese participants at a conference table can be explained by differences in orientation toward time usage and by certain cultural factors. Kume says that Japanese time orientations are "present-oriented, circular thinking, gradual build-up, and group loyalty," while American time orientations are "future-oriented, linear thinking, sense of urgency, and individualism."[9]

One American manager working for a Japanese multinational company observed that Japanese managers seldom disagree with others:"If I talk to another American, at least we would argue or discuss back and forth for ten, fifteen minutes about something until he really understands it. But we don't have much back and forth between Japanese and Americans. Japanese would, sort of, agree before that."[10]

As the above statement shows, the Japanese would rather reach a decision outside the conference room than have open and honest discussions. If differences surface, the Japanese would wait until unanimity of opinion is reached or suggest tentative agreements that will need to be confirmed in subsequent meetings. They almost never make hasty decisions to save time or meet deadlines.

Japanese businessmen also use decision-making criteria different from those used by Western businessmen. De Mente says that Japanese culture compels the Japanese to think subjectively as in "fuzzy logic" that takes unknown, irrational, and unpredictable factors into consideration.

> Westerners go all out to make rational, logical presentations, as briefly and concisely as possible. They presume that if a presentation is, in fact, rational and logical, which includes the belief that it makes good sense to both parties, that it will result in a quick, positive response. But Japanese perception of what is acceptable and desirable, even what is understandable, does not begin and end with objective reasoning. It begins and often ends with a very personal, emotional reaction that takes into account every individual involved in the discussions or who might be involved in the project if it is implemented."[11]

Obviously, the above observation does not apply to all situations, but it is necessary to recognize that "Japanese logic" is not the same as the Western logic derived from traditional Aristotelian principles. It is easy for Westerners to win an argument and lose a deal with the Japanese.

Participating in a Business Meeting

Successful participation in a decision-making meeting involving Japanese businessmen requires different strategies of communication based on good understanding of Japanese culture, social customs, and business practices. A productive international business meeting calls for careful planning, good leadership, and active participation of the participants. If the meeting is to be held in Japan, the chair must work out specific strategies far in advance. He must know the exact purpose of the meeting, select his team members, plan the agenda, and coordinate with the Japanese side.*

Chairing a business meeting in Japan has cultural constraints that need to be dealt with. Seating should be strictly according to each participant's relative status, not by work group or area of specialization. The order of speaking and of asking questions should also be based on the relative status of the Japanese representatives. It is an insult to seat people indiscriminately and to ask anyone to speak up; instead the highest-ranked person should be asked to respond first. If he does not wish to answer the question himself, he will appoint one of the subordinates to respond. It is a serious mistake to direct questions to a younger Japanese participant simply because he has an excellent command of English or technical expertise.

In a typical Japanese-American business meeting conducted in English, American participants tend to talk too much, their Japanese counterparts, too little. The chairperson must control the flow of communication from both sides and not allow the meeting to degenerate into a one-sided discussion. At the same time, he should be careful not to embarrass any Japanese participant by forcing him to speak if he is unwilling or not prepared to speak.

---

* Refer to chapter 5 for detailed information regarding selecting team members and making an agenda.

The chairperson's responsibilities in conducting a business meeting with the Japanese can be summarized as follows:

1. Start the meeting by make opening remarks and greetings. In the Western cultural context, the chairperson is expected to be humorous and informal; in the Japanese cultural context, he is expected to be formal and reserved.

2. Briefly explain the purpose and the agenda of the meeting.

3. Come in prepared and introduce each member with his proper title, special professional qualifications, and the subject he has been assigned to cover. Be very careful not to mispronounce Japanese names and titles.

4. Control the flow of communication from both sides and facilitate equal participation. Make allowance for language difficulty of the Japanese participants and give more time to them when they respond in English. Allow side-talk in Japanese among the Japanese participants if it seems needed.

5. Keep the group on course by following the agenda as much as possible, but be flexible if the Japanese side does not strictly follow the agenda.

6. Summarize and clarify the major items of discussion from time to time during the meeting. If certain English words or expressions seem difficult for the Japanese to understand, rephrase or use simpler expressions to avoid misunderstandings.

7. Mediate and solve any conflicts and rivalries and maintain an amicable and cooperative atmosphere for the meeting. (As the Japanese are sensitive to moods or feelings, they may stop participating if interpersonal conflicts appear.)

8. Help the participants reach mutually agreeable decisions by consensus. Never force decisions on the Japanese side by majority rule.

Participants to a business meeting in Japan also need to be sensitive and understand how Japanese participants will behave during the meeting. The Japanese are hesitant to voice strong personal opinions. They often use indirect and ambiguous ways of communicating when they are forced to openly make objections or negative comments. At the same time, they also worry about making themselves look foolish by speaking out in poor English or saying the wrong thing at the wrong time.

Another common frustration for Westerners trying to quickly finish a business deal in Japan is that they are often asked to repeat the same presentation for different groups of people who may or may not be directly involved in the decision to be made. In some instances, there will be "observers" sitting silently inside the meeting room and taking notes or just listening. They are not usually introduced to the visiting Western participants. They may be outsiders such as bankers or government officials or junior staff members who are being given "live training sessions" on intercultural negotiation. Westerners may feel annoyed by the presence of these people, but they should not ask the Japanese side to openly identify them. If they really want to know who these people are, they can ask someone in private.

If the Japanese businessman chairs the meeting, he may not look as skillful and assertive as his Western counterpart. He will neither lead the discussion nor control participation according to the common Western practice of conducting a business meeting. Japanese participants will most likely read what they have prepared in advance rather than freely discussing issues at hand.

The responsibilities of Western participants are as follows:

1. Find out the exact purpose of the meeting, collect necessary data and information; prepare visual aids such as charts, graphs, figures or slides, and handouts in Japanese; and prepare the presentation according to the chairperson's specific instructions. Because the Japanese side naturally wants written materials for future analysis, it is important to provide as much information as possible in printed form.

2. Attend the meeting with an open mind and flexible attitude. Be patient even if the Japanese participants do

not respond immediately. Never try to help them with their English by putting words into their mouths.

3. Be patient and listen politely even if the Japanese participants speak in broken English. Never judge the business acumen or qualifications of anyone by his language competency.

4. Respect the different points of view or different interpretations of the same issue. Refrain from dominating the discussion and trying to win arguments.

5. Maintain the group-centered attitude and assist the chairman in running the meeting efficiently.

131

Understanding the dynamics of decision making is very important. Especially in business meetings with the Japanese, group decision-making processes do not necessarily go in an orderly and rational fashion. The Japanese participants often ramble, discuss irrelevant matters, and evade touchy questions. When they meet for the first time, they are initially uneasy and hesitant. They tend to speak politely and tentatively and to engage in small talk. They are quick to agree with each other and are willing to laugh at jokes that are not even funny. The time required for releasing this primary tension depends on the composition of the group, the status relationships among the group members, and the nature of the decision they are seeking. More time may be required if there are great differences in status, age, occupational interests or specialization, and cultural backgrounds.

Generally speaking, the Japanese are subjective and personal and tend to spend much more time in releasing primary social tension. In contrast, Americans are inclined to be more objective and less personal in their attitudes toward business dealings and spend less time for this purpose.

Once the primary social tension has been released, the group is ready to work on the task at hand. They must implicitly agree on the group's hierarchical structure and roles, apart from the formal status roles assigned by the organizational hierarchy and agenda. Because all members strive for recognition of their personal and professional qualifications, both personality clashes and role conflicts inevitably occur. Participants all have a personal stake in the decision and fight to protect their own interests.

At this second stage, secondary social tensions arise from actual confrontations over specific issues. If the secondary social tensions rise above an acceptable level of tolerance or threshold of discomfort, unhappy participants will stop contributing to the group effort. The Japanese tend to be more sensitive than Westerners to secondary social tensions and will become ambiguous and noncommital and may even disdainfully withdraw from the discussion. Substantive task-oriented discussions will be halted, and the group decision-making process will come to a standstill. If this happens, the chairperson should call for a break for coffee or tea so that the participants have a chance to informally iron out the possible causes of such tensions. Only after social tensions subside below everyone's level of tolerance should the chairperson call the meeting back to order.

Time is one of the most critical factors influencing group dynamics in decision making. Although Japanese businessmen value time as much as their Western counterparts, they are less concerned with the pressure of deadlines, and they have a strong aversion to being rushed into making decisions. Time-conscious Americans will often find themselves in an awkward situation if they insist that the Japanese make quick decisions. If they pressure the Japanese side persistently, they may get a quick decision on the spot, but this decision will be overturned or ignored later.

Finally, taking accurate minutes of a business meeting is important to avoid misunderstandings. In some cases, the Japanese side may ask for permission to use a tape recorder or video recorder to record the entire proceedings of a business meeting conducted in English. Although this is a cumbersome method of taking minutes, Japanese participants will feel more comfortable if they can listen to the recordings again later. If Westerners feel uncomfortable about this recording of the entire meeting, they should try to help the Japanese side take good notes by repeating the important points of every agreement in simple English. They can even volunteer to take the minutes and give the Japanese participants a copy for their record.

American businesspeople often ask their Japanese counterparts to sign and return a copy of the minutes to have them confirm all the items of an agreement. While this is a good business practice in the United States, it can be misinterpreted as an imposition or sign of distrust by the Japanese because they consider *kuchiyakusoku* (verbal gentlemen's agreements) and *funiki* (atmosphere of the meeting) just as important as written documentary evidence. They will sign the copy without carefully reading it and complain later when problems arise.

In summary, it is extremely important that Western businesspeople realize that they may need to make concessions to the Japanese style of making decisions and conducting business meetings in order to get along in Japan.

chapter **7**

Public Speaking and Presentations

International businesspeople are frequently called upon to make speeches for various professional and civic organizations. They are also asked to make oral presentations to customers, peers, and higher management. Public speaking can be an effective means of reaching a large number of people in one setting, and making presentations is an excellent means of introducing technical information. The tradition of public speaking in the West dates back to the days of Aristotle (384–322 B.C.), and public speaking is taught in all institutions of higher learning in Western countries. Many Western businesspeople are excellent speakers, and they have no problem in making speeches and presentations to audiences with similar cultural backgrounds. However, it is a mistake to assume that the Western style of speaking is also suitable for Japanese audiences. The Western style may sound too aggressive and argumentative for Japanese listeners. The active hand gestures and body movements that are encouraged in the West may be considered impolite by the Japanese because they do not share the same traditions of public speaking.

In Japan, the teaching of public speaking was first introduced in the early 1870s by Yukichi Fukuzawa.[1] He promoted the art of public speaking by demonstrating it before various groups. He also published many books and articles to promote public speaking and Western learning. However, the study of public speaking did not flourish in Japan because the Japanese people had lived for centuries in a feudalistic society where public debate on democratic ideals was forbidden. In their hierarchical society where politeness and humility were encouraged, public display of one's intelligence and expertise was considered inappropriate. Even today, public-speaking courses are not a part of the curricula of secondary and postsecondary education in Japan. This does not mean that the Japanese do not engage in public speaking, but it means that their style of public speaking must conform to Japanese social customs and conventions.

Western speakers must understand different Japanese cultural expectations so that they can make necessary adjustments and modifications in what they say and how they speak to a Japanese audience. They must pay more attention to the purpose, occasion, and audience and must organize and deliver a speech in a culturally acceptable manner in Japan.

Purpose, Occasion, and Audience Analysis

No speaker should accept a request for public speaking without first learning about the purpose, occasion, and audience. These variables dictate how the speaker should organize and deliver his speech. He must find out whether the speech is to inform, persuade, motivate, inspire, impress, control, instruct, commemorate, or entertain. He also should know what the occasion is so that he can give an appropriate speech.

An American business executive asked to give an informative speech must find out more detailed information before accepting the request. He must ask what the purpose of this meeting is. If it is a seminar on investing in the United States sponsored by the U.S. Department of Commerce, he needs to prepare a well-organized speech with the most current trade information and statistics. If it is a semisocial occasion such as a business luncheon forum or a commemorative dinner party, he ought to be making a less serious speech with some humor. He is expected to inform and entertain at the same time. If the occasion is the anniversary party of a joint-venture contract signing, he should give a speech appropriate for this milestone. If it is a classroom situation at a Japanese university, he needs to change his speech accordingly even if he speaks on the same subject.

Once the purpose and the occasion of the speaking engagement become clear, the speaker must make an earnest effort to analyze the audience. One approach to audience analysis is called "demographic audience analysis." This analysis is based on the assumption that demographic characteristics of the members of an audience such as age, sex, marital status, occupation, socioeconomic status, political party preference, religion, and ethnic and cultural background will influence the way they respond to a message. It is always useful to find out the average age or the age range of the audience. It can be assumed that older people are generally conservative and more experienced, while younger people are more liberal but less experienced. Older people may also be more pragmatic, cautious, and reluctant to change than younger ones, who tend to be more idealistic, optimistic, and adventurous. As a general rule, a young audience will respond to challenges and exciting new ideas while an older audience will respond more favorably to appeals to tradition and to moderate reforms with good practical justifications. Age may also indicate the audience's professional and social status. The speaker is naturally required to make a very polished speech to a group of older Japanese business executives and give a less formal speech to a group of young Japanese college students.

It can also help to know if one is to speak to an audience that is made up primarily of men or of women. It is often suggested that men are generally logical and analytical, women, emotional and subjective. Japanese men tend to stress national and international economics, career advancement, and interest in sports, while Japanese women are more concerned about education, health care, family affairs, and social justice. It is also important to remember that risque humor and sexist language are often considered taboo in mixed audiences. In addition, married men and women have different personal concerns and interests from those of single men and women, who are still free of family obligations.

Occupation, socioeconomic status, political party preference, and religion are other important factors to consider. People

137

in business and industry, government service, and education have different values, attitudes, and preoccupations. Japanese business-men are well informed about the world economy and interna-tional politics, while Japanese government officials are aloof and conservative in their attitudes. Japanese teachers are more conserv-ative and hesitant to take on new challenges than their Western counterparts. The personal values of well-educated, upper- and middle-class people are different from those of less-educated, lower-class people. Naturally, a speaker is expected to talk about highly intellectual subjects and demonstrate his expertise and knowledge to an audience with high socioeconomic status, but he should avoid talking about technical subjects using technical jargon to a group of nonspecialists. Personal comments on politics should be made with care, because favorable comments on one political party can be taken as negative comments about another political party. An astute speaker should avoid making strong comments on religion as well. The Japanese usually worship both Shinto gods and Buddhist saints, and some of them attend Christian churches.

Ethnic and cultural backgrounds are important factors to recognize when speaking to Japanese audiences. Because the Japanese are ethnocentric and proud of their cultural heritage, Western speakers may cause unnecessary interpersonal friction and embarrassment if they make prejudicial statements against Japan.

Another method of analyzing the audience is called "pur-pose-oriented analysis." It attempts to find out why the members of an audience want to listen to the speech. Every member of the audience has his or her own purpose or expectation when coming to listen to a certain speaker. The speaker cannot take it for grant-ed that whatever he talks about will be acceptable to the entire audience. He must try to provide the audience with the informa-tion and data they are interested in. For example, if the American Chamber of Commerce in Tokyo sponsors a seminar on American business laws and taxation, the audience may include several top executives of Japanese multinational companies, high-level bureau-crats, business magazine reporters, and tax accountants. They all want to hear about those aspects of American business and tax laws that they consider important. Knowing in advance the different reasons why various members of the audience are attending the seminar will allow the speaker to design his speech to satisfy their respective needs.

Finally, the speaker also needs to know the level of the audience's expertise. If the audience knows nothing about the subject, he should explain basic ideas in simple language. On the other hand, if the audience is a group of professionals or experts on the subject, he should make his speech sufficiently challenging and informative with the most recent and reliable information and data.

Choosing a Topic

When the speaker has completed the audience analysis, he will have to decide his topic. At times the problem of choosing a topic is solved by the person or the organization that has invited him to speak, but he will still have to define exactly what he is going to talk about. He may be assigned too broad a topic or he himself may have too many things he wants to talk about under the assigned topic. He may also have to focus his own ideas and interests on that topic. There are three basic criteria to consider in choosing a topic:

1. Is it appropriate for the speaker? He should have enough knowledge and experience on the topic to qualify him to speak. He must be interested in the topic, because his enthusiasm and interest will be inevitably communicated to his audience. In addition, he should be able to collect necessary information and data to support his speech and his contentions objectively.

2. Is the topic suitable for the audience? The speaker will need to find topic that matches the audience's interest because his primary goal is to satisfy the audience's needs and expectations. If the audience is made up of several groups with different demographic characteristics, he must attempt to satisfy the various groups' needs and expectations by talking about topics of each one's interests and concerns.

3. Is it appropriate for the occasion and the allotted time? In almost all instances, the occasion dictates the topic. A

joyous topic should be chosen for a happy occasion, and a serious topic for a study session. It is important to note that the allotted time influences the topic. It is self-defeating to pick a topic that requires a considerable time to explain when only five or ten minutes are allotted for the speech.

Collecting Supporting Information

A good speaker conducts thorough research and collects supporting information no matter how experienced and knowledgeable he may be. Not only must he know about the topic from his viewpoint, but he must also know it from the audience's perspective. Knowing the audience's viewpoint is critical when a speaker of one culture is speaking to an audience of another culture. For example, an American government official talking to a group of Japanese businessmen about the trade imbalance with Japan may view this problem as an "economic invasion" or "trade war," but the Japanese may see it as nothing more than an "extremely successful penetration of Japanese goods into American consumer markets."

There are several forms of evidence and support for a speech such as statistics, examples, testimony, analogies, and explanations:

Statistics are numerical listings or groupings summarize many instances or occurrences. They are essential for informative speeches and very useful supporting evidence for persuasive arguments. However, statistical information should be translated into easy-to-understand terms for the audience. If statistics are used in a speech, it is extremely important to present them in Japanese standards of measurement or the metric system. Dollars, feet, miles, and pounds must be translated into yen, centimeters, kilometers, and kilograms because American measurements are meaningless to the Japanese audience. It is also important to clearly identify the sources of any statistics. The Japanese tend to have blind confidence in the official statistics provided by governmental offices and major banks' research departments. Members of a Japanese audience are likely to ask for printed statistical tables so that they can reexamine the information more carefully when they return to their offices.

Examples are descriptions of events, instances, or experiences, either real or hypothetical. Examples can be used effectively to explain a specific problem, situation, or condition that is difficult to describe verbally. The severe problem of air pollution in Los Angeles can be used as an example of increasing air pollution problems in big cities in Japan. The seriousness of drug abuse and juvenile delinquency among teenagers in New York can be explained by making up a hypothetical example with vivid descriptions. It must be recognized, however, that Western speakers may have a real difficulty in making suitable examples from their own experiences for Japanese audiences, whose professional and social life they do not share.

Testimony is the reporting of a person's opinion or an eyewitness's account. The person whose statement is used as testimony must be adequately qualified. He or she must be a widely recognized authority or an expert with proper qualifications. At the same time, the testimony must be acceptable and believable to the audience. For example, testimony by the U.S. ambassador to Japan on the future of U.S.-Japan relations will be seen as credible and reliable. Testimony by a famous Japanese astronaut on the feasibility of having a permanent space station will certainly be believable to the Japanese audience.

Analogies are comparisons of two things that are similar in essential characteristics. There are figurative and literal analogies. Examples of figurative analogies are "The Nikon has a lens as wide and bright as the human eye" or "Japan's judo champion is as strong as a bull." Literal analogies are comparisons of things of the same class: "The Cadillac Eldorado is Toyota's Lexus in the United States" or "Rough-water kayaking on the Colorado River is like the thrilling adventure of shooting the Hozu rapids."

Organizing the Speech

Ideas and materials in a speech must be organized in a manner that is familiar and acceptable to the particular audience to which the speech is directed. In many intercultural speech-making situations, how the speech is organized becomes a critical factor. For example, it is possible that a speech organized in a typical American pattern may not be appropriate for Japanese audiences. Consequently, it is necessary for an American speaker to adapt his speech to the Japanese audience, which has different expectations toward public speaking.

Generally speaking, a speech has three major parts: an introduction, a body, and a conclusion. The introduction gives the audience a brief preview of what the speech is about. A good introduction will help the speaker accomplish the following: (1) capture the attention and interest of all members of the audience, (2) establish rapport and credibility with the audience, (3) explain to the audience how the speech relates to their needs, (4) tell them the purpose of the speech, (5) inform them of the main topics and subtopics in a sequential order.

Opening remarks in the introduction can be a reference to the occasion, a compliment for the audience, reference to the common experience of the speaker and audience, reference to current or historical events, a startling statement, a question, a quotation, or a joke. The type of introduction depends largely upon the speaker's personal preference, the occasion, the content of the speech, and the cultural context in which the speech is given.

In Japan, it is appropriate that a speaker begin his remarks by apologizing or humbling himself. This apology is a social ritual that every Japanese speaker is expected to perform because humility is considered a virtue in the Japanese cultural context. The speaker may begin with such typical self-effacing introductory remarks as: *Takai tokoro kara ohanashi wo suru no wa kyōshuku desu ga* or "I hesitate to address you from a high place (an elevated podium), but . . ." *Watakushi nado ga minasama ni ohanashi suru no wa* or "I really don't deserve the honor of speaking to you, but . . ."

These ritualistic Japanese remarks might be misinterpreted by a Western audience as showing the speaker's lack of confidence and authority. However, the Japanese speaker is merely saying what he is expected to say in this context. This does not mean that Western speakers should use these apologetic remarks, but they ought be more conservative and formal when talking to Japanese audiences. Westerners should refrain from starting a speech with boisterous humor or excessively informal remarks as they would do in their own culture. In most instances, use of humor is unwise because humor from one culture may not be humorous in another culture. For example, an American speaker's humor is almost impossible for Japanese people to understand unless they have lived or worked among Americans for a long time. Japanese may not laugh at the speaker's joke anyway because they consider it impolite to laugh at someone who is an honored guest speaker. It is more appropriate to begin by recognizing all important people in the audience in a strict order of relative social rankings individually or as a group. The following could be a proper introductory remark to a Japanese audience:

> "Thank you for your kind introduction. President Shimada, Vice President Tanaka, Honored Guests, Ladies and Gentlemen. I am John Smith, Senior Vice President of Asia Pacific Consulting Group. It is my great pleasure and honor to be here this morning to participate in the Asian Pacific Economic Development Seminar sponsored by your esteemed organization. For the past twenty years, I have been actively involved in the study of economic developments in several Asian countries. This morning I wish to share with you my humble opinion on the dynamic economic developments in China, Vietnam, Indonesia, and Malaysia . . . "

143

The body is the main section of the speech. There are several ways to arrange the major points in the body of the speech. In choosing the most appropriate pattern of organization, the speaker should reevaluate the information obtained from the prior audience analysis, the occasion, and the purpose and adapt it to the situation and to the specific needs of the audience. A speech can be arranged in a chronological pattern, geographical pattern, topical pattern, problem-solution pattern, cause-effect pattern, and motivated sequence pattern.

The chronological pattern (also called the "time sequence pattern) is used when the speaker wishes to organize his speech in the sequence of the past, the present, and the future. This is an excellent pattern to use when talking about a company's history. For example, a speech on the company can be arranged as follows: "when the company was founded by whom, and what it was doing; what it is doing now; and what it plans to do in the future." This is an effective pattern of organization for a Japanese audience beacause Japanese businessmen are generally interested in the history or heritage of a business organization.

The Geographical pattern (also called the space sequence pattern) is suitable for such topics as geography, travel, transportation, and planning. The main points are arranged in terms of physical location, moving from east to west, from the center to the outside, or from city to city and country to country. For example, an American executive in charge of international operations can talk about several successful overseas operations in Hong Kong, Singapore, Malaysia, Thailand, and China in order of geographical positions on the map of Asia.

The topical pattern of arrangement is used for a speech that can be categorized into separate topics and subtopics. It is a convenient pattern to use when a speaker wishes to talk about various aspects of a country, company, or organization. The speaker can organize an informative speech on Hawai'i by covering such topics as Hawaiian history, geography, climate, education, industries, population, religions, and so on. Or he may arrange a persuasive speech on the bright future of an extremely successful company by introducing the most recent innovative activities in several departments such as Research and Development, Production, Accounting and Finance, Personnel, and Sales and Marketing. This is the most widely used form of speech organization.

The problem-solution pattern can be used effectively for persuasive speeches intended to propose new solutions or changes. This approach requires that a speaker first define the problem, then discuss advantages and disadvantages of several solutions, and finally advocate one solution as the best, using reliable information and data. For example, if a speaker wishes to persuade top management to purchase a new computer system, he has to present the seriousness of the problem caused by the old computer system currently in service and suggest alternative solutions such as repairing, upgrading, or buying a new system.

Finally, the best solution—buying the new computer system—is advocated, based on the thorough analysis of the merits and demerits of all solutions.

The cause-effect pattern is based on a chain of cause-effect relationships and the assumption that elimination of certain causes will bring about desirable effects. The speaker who uses this pattern must first establish that the desirable effects are directly related to the causes their audience is concerned about. Then, he advocates that the elimination of the causes will produce desirable effects in the future. For example, a speech on the problem of international drug cartels can be organized as follows: "The illegal activities of international drug cartels are undermining the social mores and promoting violent crimes in all industrialized nations; the industrialized nations of the world are suffering from the rampant illegal activities of the drug cartels; therefore, to regain social stability and establish drug-free international communities, all the industrialized nations must pool their resources to eliminate these drug cartels."

The motivated sequence pattern (also called the psychological progression pattern) is considered the most effective pattern of organization for persuasive speeches. The sequence has five steps that follow the psychology of persuasion, and it is designed to motivate the audience to move toward immediate acceptance of the speaker's appeal. It consists of an attention step, need step, satisfaction step, visualization step, and action step, and each of these steps has specific functions:

1. Attention step—gain the audience's attention and arouse interest by showing the importance of the topic, making a startling statement, or telling a dramatic story.

2. Need step—show that there is a serious problem with the existing situation and that changes are urgently needed.

3. Satisfaction step—satisfy the needs (newly created by the speaker) by providing a viable solution to the problem. Support the proposed solution by offering enough examples, statistics, and testimony.

4. Visualization step—provide a vivid image of what will happen if the audience adopts the solution.

5. Action step—convince the audience to take immediate action.

Transitions are words, phrases, sentences, or rhetorical questions that join subtopics and ideas in a speech. They are like signposts, and used when a speaker completes a main idea or a subtopic before moving to the next one; they show the audience the connections among the subtopics. A transitional statement is also used when the speaker moves from the introduction to the body of the speech. Transitions include such phrases as "If I may illustrate my point, . . . ," "This point raises another questions of . . . ," "Now, let us look at . . . ," "In other words, . . . ," "In contrast, . . . ," and "In summary, . . ."

Clear transitions are mandatory in all speech making. This is especially true when speaking to Japanese audiences whose English is limited. When speaking through an interpreter, easy-to-identify transitions are absolutely necessary because the interpreter needs to follow the flow of the speech and make timely adjustments. In a sequential interpreting session, the interpreter depends on clear transitions or verbal cues given by the speaker to start interpreting what the speaker has just said.

In the conclusion, the final part of the speech, the speaker summarizes or restates the main ideas to ensure that members of the audience will understand the message and respond to it as the speaker has intended. The conclusion takes various forms depending on the purpose of the speech. It could be a summary or recapitulation of the main idea, a challenge, an appeal, or a quotation by a famous authority. It should also reflect the purpose of the speech and the introductory remarks. It is good to remember that Japanese speakers always end a speech by thanking the audience. The most common ending is *Goseichō arigatō gozaimashita* or "Thank you for your patience." This statement again reflects the self-humility that was shown in the introduction.

Use of Visual Aids and Handouts

Visual aids are absolutely necessary when speaking to Japanese audiences because the visuals can supplement verbal messages that could otherwise be difficult for them to understand. Because people now live in a visual age, adding visual images also improves clarity, interest, retention, and credibility. The most common forms of visual aids are objects, models, photographs, drawing, charts, graphs, figures, diagrams, transparencies, slides, videotapes, computer-generated graphics, and handouts. These visual aids are extremely useful in presenting statistical data, numerical comparisons, trends, increases and decreases, and pictorial descriptions. However, poor handling of them can become a hindrance rather than an aid to effective speaking.

A good speaker should know how to prepare and present various types of visual aids. Objects are excellent visual aids to use when discussing equipment, tools, and machines. For example, when talking about preventing injuries in football games, the speaker can show various types of safety equipment currently used by American professional football teams to demonstrate their merits. Models can be used when actual objects are too large or too heavy. For example, a small-scale model of the Concorde, a supersonic jetliner, might be used.

Photographs are effective visual aids for showing objects, people, and sports activities. They can be shown in slides, enlarged to poster-size prints, or copied onto transparencies by a color copier. Diagrams and sketches, which are inexpensive and easy to make, are alternatives to photographs. Graphs are a good way to simplify and clarify statistics. Line graphs are used to show trends, pie charts to show distribution, and bar graphs to show comparisons. Charts are particularly useful for summarizing large blocks of information, and different colors can be used for lines or phrases to accentuate the differences.

Transparencies prepared in advance can be shown with an overhead projector, or blank transparencies can be placed on the projector so that a speaker can write down main points while speaking. Slides can be effective when talking about scenic spots, architecture, and art objects. Videotapes are more cumbersome because they require playback equipment. Videotapes also require careful editing and handling. It is a good idea to dub the videotapes with a Japanese-language narration so that Japanese audiences do not have to struggle with a fast-paced English narration. Recently, computer-generated graphics have become popular in place of other traditional visual aids. These graphics can include anything from simple diagrams to sophisticated charts and graphs. If notations and explanations are written in Japanese, all of these visual aids will be invaluable in facilitating good communication with Japanese audiences.

There are several tips for using visual aids effectively: (1) Prepare visual aids well ahead of time and use them while practicing the speech. (2) Make sure that visual aids are large enough for everyone in the audience to see. (3) Avoid passing out any of the visual aids and other printed material to ensure that everyone is listening to the speech instead of looking at the printed visual aids. (4) Display applicable visual aids only while discussing them. (5) Maintain good eye contact with the audience and do not look at the visual aids except for a few seconds to check that they are shown correctly.

Methods of Speech Delivery

Writing a speech and preparing visual aids is only one half of the task of speech making. The speech must be delivered effectively to complete the other half of the task. There are basically four methods of speech delivery: impromptu speaking, manuscript speaking, extemporaneous speaking, and memorized speaking.

For impromptu speaking speakers make no formal preparation until a few minutes before they begin to talk. They may jot down a few words or ideas, but they make spur-of-the moment or off-the-cuff remarks or statements. Americans are adept at impromptu speaking, but they should be careful not to make the blunder of making a speech too casual and informal when addressing a Japanese audience.

Extemporaneous speaking requires that speakers plan carefully and rehearse several times until they feel confident that they can deliver the speech without difficulty. They may use notes to remind themselves of the sequence and main points, but they do not need to follow exactly what they have planned to say. They can be flexible in the use of alternative words and phrases. This is considered the best method of delivery because the speaker can maintain good eye contact and receive direct feedback from the audience.

Manuscript speaking is based on meticulously worded manuscripts. This method of speaking is highly recommended for important speeches such as a presentation to the Japan Federation of Employers or a speech for the Japanese Press Club on sensitive trade issues where a wrong choice of words or phrases can cause serious misunderstandings. In such situations, the manuscript is usually given to the members of the audience in advance so that they can study it beforehand. Speakers reading from a manuscript may suffer from three disadvantages: (1) They cannot maintain good eye contact with the audience. (2) They sound monotonous as they are reading the manuscript. (3) They cannot spontaneously adjust and respond to audience reactions. They can alleviate some of these problems if they have their manuscript printed out in large type and triple spaced, and make notations in different colored pens to indicate places of emphasis and pauses. This is the most common method of delivery among Japanese speakers because they are extremely worried about making mistakes in public-speaking situations.

Memorized speaking is difficult for ordinary speakers because they must memorize an entire speech and deliver it with-out any mistakes. Inexperienced speakers may forget certain key words or start with the wrong beginning sentence, thereby losing their train of thought and causing an embarrassing situation. To avoid such a disaster, speakers are advised to hold onto a few notes outlining the main points.

149

Voice and Vocal Habits

Voice is important because it reflects the speaker's attitudes, feel-ings, enthusiasm, confidence, and competence. Good delivery also means that the speaker can be heard, can be clearly understood, and has no annoying vocal habits. Native speakers of English may not have problems with articulation, intonation, stress patterns, and pitch, but they may need to adjust their volume and rate of speak-ing when addressing a Japanese audience.

Many Japanese complain that Americans speak too loudly and too rapidly and do not enunciate clearly. Because speaking too loudly is considered impolite and boastful in the Japanese public-speaking context, shouting should never be used even in a highly charged emotional situation. Speakers must also slow down con-siderably and articulate each word and every phrase very clearly. Common vocal habits such as "an' uh," "uh huh," "wha chuma call," "you know," "you see," and "anyways" should be avoided because they are very distracting sounds. In addition, colloquial expressions and slang should never be used when speaking to non-native speakers of English.

Facial Expressions, Gestures, Posture, and Body Movements

The nonverbal aspect of speech making is just as important as the verbal message. Speakers communicate nonverbally their inner feelings such as attitudes, enthusiasm, disinterest, satisfaction, or dissatisfaction. They can emphasize, negate, or even contradict their verbal messages through nonverbal behaviors.

Facial expressions such as smiling and laughing are the most visible and important nonverbal behaviors. In public-speaking situations, Americans are affable and friendly, wearing big smiles. In contrast, the Japanese are more reserved and stoic in the same situations because they are expected to be formal and serious. Consequently, overly friendly or casual facial expressions may offend Japanese listeners, especially when the speakers are discussing serious topics or sensitive issues. Jokes or funny anecdotes, often used in social situations in the West to break interpersonal tensions, are considered rude and inappropriate in Japan. This does not mean that Japanese people dislike pleasant facial expressions, but they may become suspicious of a speaker's trustworthiness if the speaker appears overly affable and too friendly. It is advisable to maintain a certain amount of modesty and formality in public-speaking situations in Japan.

Gestures—using the hands to describe the shape of something, pointing a finger, using a fist or arms—are used to augment the verbal message. Using gestures in public speaking requires vitality, proper timing, and coordination with the spoken message. Although gestures are effective as a means of reinforcing the spoken message, they should not be used excessively or aimlessly. Wrong and untimely gestures are not only distracting, but also annoying and destructive. For example, speakers should never use the index finger to point at the members of Japanese audiences. They should also avoid big hand gestures such as throwing their arms up high and waving their hands.

Postures and body movements are also important in public-speaking situations. Proper speaking postures and body movements vary among cultures. In Japan, a self-effacing low posture *(teishisei)* is appropriate, but in the West, an erect posture showing self-confidence is called for. Japanese speakers usually remain standing behind the podium on the platform, while American speakers will come down in front of the podium and move about closer to the audience. They may even walk back and forth like a talk-show host and address members of the audience individually. These normal Western behaviors will be viewed as impolite and distracting in Japan. Westerners must recognize that they need to restrain themselves and behave conservatively when speaking to a Japanese audience.

151

Tips for Effective Presentations

Making oral presentation in multinational business contexts differs considerably from other types of public speaking. The presentation usually has more narrowly defined and specific objectives, and it is given to a much smaller number of people. The basic purpose of the presentation is to secure a favorable response from the executives and managers who have the decision-making power. It can be used for recommending acceptance of a budget, making a proposal for innovations, and proposing a solution for serious personnel management problems. There are specific requirements in preparing and delivering a presentation to accomplish its intended purpose.

Audience analysis for a presentation requires that a speaker investigate the specific background information of each member of the audience such as current status and position, preferences, interests, responsibility and authority, personal stake, attitudes, and personality. Suppose that the audience is made up of the vice president of finance, the director of marketing, the manager of the human resources department, and the supervisor of facilities management. The speaker must check out each person's background so that he can prepare and deliver his presentation accordingly. Another aspect of this audience analysis is to accurately assess which member is the actual decision maker. The speaker must always remember that it is necessary to persuade the most powerful person and win his support first when speaking to a small group of Japanese executives or managers. It is not easy to find out to whom the presentation should be directed, however, just by looking at the relative ranks of the members of an audience. It is possible that the highest-ranked Japanese executive could be present just as an observer, and his immediate subordinate actually has the decision-making power. In some instances, the speaker will be asked to make the same presentation to a few other groups if the initial group members are not totally satisfied and want others to get involved.

Research for a presentation should be extensive and complete. Because important decisions will be made on the information and data given in the presentation, the speaker must conduct thorough research and must collect enough accurate and factual supporting materials to advocate his contentions. At the same time, he must recognize that some members of the audience may have considerable professional knowledge and expertise on the subject of his presentation. The most persuasive types of supporting evidence are official government statistics, current data and information from research institutes, corporate annual reports, and research reports from business consultants.

The average time for a presentation may be only twenty or thirty minutes, but the speaker must cover a lot of material within this limited period. In some cases, he will send out a packet of supporting materials to the members of the audience to look at before coming to the presentation. The presentation itself then becomes the speaker's analysis of the major points and his recommendation based on his interpretation of the pertinent information and data used in the proposal. The speaker will need to prepare a variety of visual aids to make each major point clearly and concisely. He also needs to be prepared to handle specific questions for clarification and have an open mind to receive comments and constructive criticisms.

In organizing a presentation, it is possible to use the same patterns of organization used for other public speaking. However, three basic patterns are more suitable for presentations: psychological progression pattern, open proposal pattern, and logical problem–solution pattern.[2]

The psychological progression pattern is an adaptation of Monroe's Motivated Sequence.[3] It consists of five steps to motivate the audience toward the speaker's goal: (1) arouse the audience's interest; (2) expose the problem; (3) satisfy the needs of the audience; (4) help the audience visualize the result; and (5) move the audience to act on the speaker's recommendation.

The open proposal pattern is similar to deductive reasoning, in which speakers start with a general conclusion and then provide specific reasons to support this conclusion. The speaker may urge the audience to accept the proposition on the basis of desirability, validity, practicality, morality, legality, and so on. This pattern of organization is most suitable for those listeners who are familiar with the speaker's subject. It can also be used effectively in making a new proposal or presenting a solution.

The logical problem–solution pattern is an adaptation of the reflective thinking analysis of John Dewey.[4] It is based on the assumption that a rational person tends to go through the reflective thinking process in deciding his or her solution to a complex problem. The five major steps are (1) defining a problem; (2) exploring the problem; (3) suggesting several possible solutions; (4) identifying criteria for a solution; and (5) selecting the best solution. When using this pattern, the speaker must make sure that the members of the audience will apply the same criteria for their own evaluation of the recommended solution. Application of different criteria could result in disagreement between the speaker and the listeners.

When using the above patterns of organization, the speaker must remember that these are based on traditional Western logic, and his presentations organized in this manner may sound too argumentative and combative to Japanese listeners who are not familiar with the rhetorical tradition of Western cultures. Consequently, the speaker should soften his logical arguments and provide good explanations for each major point for the Japanese audience. He may be able to win an argument easily against the Japanese, but he may have difficulty in persuading them to accept the Western logic wholeheartedly.

Delivery of a presentation is different from that of other forms of public speaking. It is characterized by a conversational style of speaking and use of report language. It should always

153

include a question-and-answer period during or after the presentation. In handling the question-and-answer period, Western speakers should know that Japanese listeners may not ask any questions. They are usually hesitant to ask questions in public because they are concerned about violating the social etiquette of speaking up. For example, a junior Japanese manager will never ask questions unless he can obtain implicit approval from his superior in the same audience. The speaker should politely ask the highest-ranked Japanese executive to respond first. If he does not have any questions himself, he may encourage one of his subordinates to respond. The speaker should also stay behind a few minutes after the presentation, because the Japanese tend to ask questions in private after others have left.

Finally, the most important tip is that the speaker talks slowly and clarify each main point one at a time. Good understanding of the content and of the specific proposal is an important prerequisite for a successful presentation.

Working for Overseas Japanese Multinationals

The rapid globalization of the Japanese economy has made a large number of Japanese companies into multinational entities that employ foreign managers, computer engineers, technical experts, factory workers, restaurant workers, and construction laborers. Many Japanese companies, particularly in labor-intensive manufacturing sectors, have established overseas subsidiaries and joint ventures to capitalize on cheap labor and to compete in local markets. Today, it is estimated that more than 750,000 local people are working for Japanese multinational companies in foreign countries. The number of these foreign workers will continue to grow as more and more Japanese companies relocate their manufacturing operations overseas.

Despite the fact that these Japanese companies provide good employment, a large percentage of foreigners have difficulty working for their Japanese employers because the Japanese companies are not truly multinational with regard to organizational structure, human resource management policies, and compensation. Because Japan has successfully attained the status of the second-strongest economic power in the world, Japanese employers feel justified in maintaining uniquely Japanese management practices with little adaptation to the changing nature of multinational operations in foreign countries. Even today Japanese companies almost never hire host nationals or third-country nationals for key managerial positions. If they do, they do not hire these foreigners as *seishain* (regular permanent employees) but only as *shokutaku* (contract employees), no matter how professionally or technically qualified they may be. In addition, most of these companies are still financing their overseas operations through branches of Japanese banks with which they have had long-term business relations. Non-Japanese managers and workers employed by Japanese multinational companies need to know the unique features of typical Japanese multinational companies and should understand several critical issues and problems that they may encounter. They also need to realize that the Japanese multinational companies are very slow in "localizing" their overseas operations even though some of these companies have already begun to adopt a more global approach.

The Corporate Structure of Japanese Multinationals

Unlike multinational corporations from Western countries, Japanese multinationals are not true multinationals with regard to their organizational structure, personnel management policies, and operation practices. They are mostly wholly owned subsidiaries under very tight control of their headquarters in Japan, and they have little autonomy in the management of local operations. These overseas subsidiaries are also considered to have subordinate status in the overall corporate structure regardless of their size or profitability. Furthermore, if the company is a large manufacturing company, it is supported by many Japanese subcontractors that have built their factories in the industrial area close to the parent company. The overseas subsidiaries even use the same system of subcontracting that they have established back in Japan so that they can continue to do business with the same subcontractors. For example, Honda America had some forty-eight of their Japanese subcontractors build their factories in the United States and continue to supply important parts to them as they had been doing in Japan.[1]

Japanese companies have a much larger number of Japanese expatriates in the management cadre than American or European companies' foreign subsidiaries, and almost all key managerial and engineering positions are occupied by Japanese managers dispatched from the parent company for a fixed period of time. In many instances, lower supervisory positions are also occupied by the Japanese expatriates. A typical organizational chart of any Japanese multinational will show that top management and supervisory positions are reserved for Japanese nationals. In those countries where governmental regulations require hiring local managers, they will usually create co-manager positions even though actual control is in the hands of the Japanese counterparts. (They are sometimes referred to as "shadow managers.")

Japanese multinational companies seem to believe that their ways of operation are far superior, particularly in the manufacturing sector. Most Japanese manufacturers introduce Japanese machinery, manufacturing methods, and typical Japanese management into their overseas operations. Sethi, Namiki, and Swanson labeled this approach "acculturation or cultural transformation approach." It calls for creating a new corporate culture within their foreign subsidiaries, because indoctrination of non-Japanese workers is a necessary precondition for the successful introduction of Japanese management practices. Non-Japanese workers are expected to quickly acquire Japanese cultural values, work ethics, and thought processes. Typically, Japanese multinationals take a number of measures to see that these expectations are met, including hiring certain types of employees, providing intensive indoctrination and education, and giving home office training to select employees.[2]

Recruitment and Indoctrination in Japanese Multinationals

Japanese multinationals carefully select and screen new employees through a series of personal interviews to ensure that new hires will have a positive attitude toward Japan and the Japanese management system. The employees are expected to have "Japanese-like" personality traits such as perseverance, obedience, discipline, loyalty, flexibility, and group-orientedness. The companies prefer to hire workers with no prior work experience because they do not wish to hire those workers who might have developed unhealthy work habits. This same hiring practice has been commonly adopted in Japan when recruiting new Japanese employees.[3]

Like their counterparts in Japan, newly recruited workers are given extensive training not only in job-related skills, but also in corporate history, traditions, and culture. During the training period of three to six months, Japanese multinationals oblige their new employees to learn the *shachōkun* (president's teachings), *sōritu no seishin* (founder's motto), and *shaka* (company song). Those companies that were established by charismatic presidents will always include in the training materials the accounts of the founder's personal philosophy of management, the initial hardships, and the subsequent glorious corporate history and traditions. These are translated into local languages and referred to frequently to instill these ideals in the minds of local employees. During the daily *chōrei* (morning pep-talk session), employees are required to recite the president's teachings and the founder's motto and to sing the company song as a part of the continuous indoctrination of the employees into Japanese corporate culture. In addition, many Japanese companies encourage the employees to study the Japanese language and culture either by providing them with in-house training courses or subsidizing tuition payment.

The Japanese multinationals also select and send employees to Japan to be trained at their headquarters for three months to one year. The aims of this training in Japan are not only to have the employees go through intensive technical training, but also to have them immerse themselves in the Japanese corporate culture. They are also expected to become personally acquainted with their Japanese counterparts and to build interpersonal networks through working together and socializing after work. Upon returning to their own jobs, they are assigned to play the role of strong advocates of the proper Japanese way of working and doing things and to teach others what they learned in Japan.

Recently, several major Japanese multinationals have begun local manager-development programs for young staff members from foreign countries. They carefully select between twenty and thirty new graduates with master's degrees or doctorates from prestigious universities in international business, finance, computer science, chemistry, or engineering. These recruits go through two or three years of intensive technical training at headquarters. They are also expected to study the Japanese language and culture during their stay in Japan. When they successfully complete this training, they will be sent back to their home countries to work as managers and supervisors in the subsidiaries of these multinationals. For example, Matsushita Electric Company has started a local manager-development program to cultivate non-Japanese management talent for their subsidiaries. Each year they recruit ten or twenty new graduates with master's degrees from prestigious American universities and give them intensive technical training and provide them with opportunities to study the Japanese language and culture as well. They will be assigned to work for Matsushita's subsidiaries in the United States, and they are expected to become "cultural bridges" between the Japanese management and American workers. This is a new program of localizing managerial staff adopted by many other Japanese multinationals such as Sony, Hitachi, Fujitsu, Toshiba, and Nippon Steel.

Transferring of the Japanese corporate culture intact has not been without problems. Fukuda reports that it has not always been feasible or effective to introduce Japanese ideologies and management practices into host countries because of differences in cultural values and social customs. He found that the attempts in the United States and Britain had largely failed because of vast differences in cultural values. Even in East Asian countries such as South Korea, Taiwan, Singapore, and Hong Kong, Japanese subsidiaries could not implement typical Japanese-style management practices. Management of the Japanese subsidiaries failed to recognize that even geographical proximity and similar racial and cultural heritage do not make other Asians think and behave exactly like the Japanese. Fukuda's research also found that the vast majority of Hong Kong Chinese did not really want to work for Japanese companies that demand total loyalty in return for job security; they would rather work for American companies, which pay them higher wages and promote them faster. He concluded that Japanese subsidiaries should modify their management approach by adopting some local customs and business practices because the Japanese style was neither applicable nor acceptable to all other Asians.[4]

Japanese Expatriate Managers and Overseas Assignments

All of the Japanese managers and supervisors assigned overseas are dispatched from the headquarters "on loan" or *shikkō*, and they continue to maintain close official ties with their former sections or departments at home. In essence, their assignments are more like a prolonged overseas business trip as they are usually expected to return to their old positions when they complete the overseas assignments. However, not all of these Japanese expatriates are happy volunteers for overseas assignments. In many instances, they are not chosen for their exceptional managerial skills or their foreign-language competence, but simply because it is their turn. They are usually given little advance notice—three months or less. They may go through an intensive language course and some cross-cultural training, but they are generally expected to prepare themselves to take on the assignment without much training. Wives and children who are to accompany these managers may receive a few orientation sessions. Fukuda found that many firms doing business abroad have not faced the problem of training Japanese expatriate managers, although almost all Japanese firms sponsor intensive language training (usually English), ranging from two months to one year in duration.[5] Major manufacturing firms and financial institutions often use employees with graduate degrees from foreign universities under a company-sponsored study-abroad program. However there are too few young employees with both good technical knowledge and familiarity of the sociocultural environment of a foreign country to cover even a fraction of all foreign assignments.

Generally speaking, Japanese expatriates belong to either the junior management group or the senior executive group. Junior managers are in their late twenties or early thirties, and sometimes they lack adequate business experience. They are assigned to overseas positions because they are still young and psychologically flexible enough to make necessary personal adjustments in a foreign environment. Quite often, they are management trainees who are being given the opportunity to learn the language and business practices during their foreign assignments. On average, they are assigned for a three-year period, although some of them may stay for five years or more. They rarely wish to remain abroad for a long time because they fear that they may lose their personal ties with those at the home office. Nakane says, "The absence or loss of tangibility from the main body for an extended period of time invariably means the erosion of all-critical social assets. . . . Group unity is maintained in the Japanese culture by strong emphasis on emotional commitment. An appeal to emotion, though most effective, requires constant face-to-face contact."[6]

The young managers worry about missing a timely opportunity to get promoted while they are away since promotion is generally based on seniority back in Japan.

Senior Japanese executives assigned abroad are usually in their mid-forties or early fifties. Prior to overseas assignments, they usually are only section chiefs or department heads at the home office. In overseas ventures they are assigned to top management positions and given big titles such as chief executive officer, president, senior vice president, and general manager. Some of the senior managers are *amakudari,* descending to an overseas subsidiary from "heaven," the home office. They are often sent down because suitable managerial positions are not available to them in Japan. They are assigned to top overseas positions not necessarily because of their exceptional professional competency, but because of their extensive personal ties with many key people at the home office. They may also have public relations skills considered convenient for entertaining important clients who will visit from Japan. In fact, those who are in their mid-fifties are given titular positions in overseas subsidiaries before their retirement as a reward for their many years of dedicated service. Consequently, even these senior managers working for overseas subsidiaries do not have the same authority and influence that their colleagues in Japan with similar managerial titles may have. In short, the overseas Japanese multinationals are neither autonomous nor semiautonomous operations, but are locked in a tight hierarchical relationship with their parent companies.

Japanese managers on foreign assignments need to cope with personal problems such as their children's education and renting their house or apartment in Japan. Providing their children with Japanese-style education in foreign countries is a serious disincentive of overseas assignment for Japanese managers. Those junior managers with young children usually send them to the overseas Japanese schools established by the Japanese Ministry of Education and the Ministry of Foreign Affairs; these are financed by donations from local Japanese businesses and by tuition income. There are many such schools in foreign cities with large Japanese populations. If there is no such school, these expatriates will unwillingly send the children to local schools. If they do so, they will use the service of special schools that provide Japanese education on weekends (these schools are called *hoshū gakkō* or *kyōiku juku).* The mothers may also tutor the children at home on

Japanese subjects using school materials from Japan. Many Japanese parents send their junior-high-school-age children back to Japan in care of their relatives, who will look after the children's educational needs. It is extremely important for them to be able to enroll in Japanese schools back home when they return.

The senior managers may have high-school or college-age children who do not wish to disrupt their education in Japan by joining their fathers. It is particularly important that the high-school-age children study hard to prepare themselves for college entrance examinations. The college-age children will not want to miss the opportunities to establish lifelong friendships and personal connections among their classmates at a Japanese university by transferring to a foreign university. They are also concerned about missing a timely job-hunting opportunity in Japan if they are away in the junior or senior year. Consequently, some of the senior managers are forced to take *tanshin funin* or "assignment without family members" and lead a lonely life overseas because their wives need to stay back in Japan and care for the children.

Still another disincentive for Japanese managers facing overseas assignment is that they will have to rent their house or apartment. Almost all Japanese homeowners loathe renting their family homes to strangers because they have invested a lot of money in them. In addition, rental laws in Japan are disproportionately in favor of renters. The renters can ask for a large sum of *tachinoki ryō* or "relocation charge" from the landlords and even refuse to move out if they can prove that it will cause a hardship.

Compensation and Managerial Functions

All Japanese expatriate managers are given generous compensation while they are on overseas assignments. Because of the strong yen *(endaka)*, even their ordinary compensation could be a substantial amount. In some instances they receive two separate paychecks—one paycheck from the overseas subsidiary they work for, which covers necessary living expenses plus an overseas allowance, and another paycheck given to them in Japan, which could amount to base pay plus semiannual bonuses. Many major Japanese multinationals give overseas managers so-called net pay after taxes to ensure that they have ample income to lead a comfortable personal life. In addition, even junior expatriate managers and supervisors are provided with company housing, a company car, an entertainment expense account, a special overseas allowance, an educational allowance, and home leave. Those senior managers assigned to top management positions receive good pay and bonuses, and they are usually given home leave every two years if the duration of their assignments is more than three years. They are provided with a plush condominium or a big house to live in, a full-size deluxe company car, and memberships at exclusive country clubs and prestigious civic clubs; a very generous expense account is provided because they must personally take care of a large number of important visitors from Japan, including top management from the home office. These luxuries are essential in keeping a good corporate image in the local business community.

163

The case of C. Itoh and Company (America) is a good example of this particular Japanese practice:

> The Japan staff also received a family allowance—30 percent of the base salary for the wife, 10 percent for each child of school age and above, and 5 percent for each child under school age, not to exceed 50 percent of the base salary. The allowance was paid, if necessary, directly to the family members who remained in Japan. Itoh (Japan) paid an allowance in yen to children of Japan staff attending college in Japan. . . . This family allowance was not available to American staff, since their salaries are paid according to what is practiced generally in the U.S. business environment.[7]

The apparent disparity between the compensation and allowances given to *honsha-haken* (home-office-dispatched) Japanese managers and supervisors and that given to *genchi saiyō* (locally hired managers and employees)* has often been a cause of

---

* *"Genchi saiyō"* refers to those people hired locally as local employees based on local labor practices. They do not enjoy the extra benefits that are given to those dispatched from Japan. The majority of them are Japanese nationals or other Asians who are either naturalized citizens or legal residents of the country in which they are working.

interpersonal jealousy, dissatisfaction, or hard feelings. This disparity is even more disturbing for those locally hired Japanese expatriates, because they are paid much less and given fewer allowances. They feel that they are more familiar with local culture and social customs, language, and business conditions than their Japan-dispatched counterparts. Besides, they claim to have a long-term commitment and a strong sense of loyalty to the Japanese subsidiary they work for.

Interpersonal Relationships between Japanese and Local Staff

The general Japanese attitude toward foreigners can cause serious conflicts and psychological strain between Japanese managers and local staff in Japanese multinationals. The Japanese managers tend to believe that Japanese management practices are culture-unique and that no foreigners will ever fully understand the proper Japanese way of doing business. Because almost all of them had little or no experience working with non-Japanese colleagues or subordinates before, they often lack cross-cultural communication skills and are at a loss as to what to do, especially when they have to supervise Westerners. At the same time, they are afraid of being identified by their colleagues in Japan as *gaikoku boke* (foreign country fool) or *gaijin kabure* (quasi-foreigner)—that is, someone who has acquired the bad habits of a "peculiar" foreign country. They feel the strong need to stay "Japanese" even if they think that they should adopt or adapt to the proper ways of doing things in a foreign cultural environment. They also realize that their career advancement is more often tied to how they are viewed and evaluated by the superiors and colleagues at the home office than to good performance at the overseas posts. This psychological ambivalence causes the development of *koshikake konjō* or "temporary-stay mentality" that is not only counterproductive but also detrimental to maintaining good morale among the locally hired staff.

The poor attitude and behavior of Japanese superiors often causes difficulties for local employees of Japanese multinationals. The most disturbing matter for local managers and supervisors is that they will not be trusted or given top managerial positions no matter how competent and qualified they may be. Even if they are given top positions and big titles, they will not be given any real authority and power to make independent decisions. They will be closely watched by the home-office-dispatched managers, who are assigned to guard against any actions that are not approved by the home office. These "shadow managers" keep a close watch on everything and anything that is going on by requiring the foreign managers to submit oral and written reports frequently. They are always having informal communication sessions in Japanese with fellow-Japanese expatriates, and they make frequent reports to their superiors in Japan. Non-Japanese managers working for Japanese multinationals find it difficult to cope with this situation, especially if they are accustomed to having open communication and taking independent action.

165

Another disturbing matter is that the Japanese managers and supervisors do not mingle with their non-Japanese counterparts. They continue to socialize with each other after work and even on weekends and discuss important business decisions informally among themselves. Unless the local staff can speak good Japanese and become part of the socializing group, they will be left out of the informal but crucial communication networks.

The Japanese managers also spend a lot of time entertaining frequent visitors from Japan, taking them sightseeing, golfing, dining, nightclubbing, and shopping. Local staff often complain that their Japanese superiors put a priority on socializing because they entertain their guests during the workday.

Expatriate Japanese managers develop strong attachments to local Japanese communities. Those Japanese managers stationed in large cities with a large Japanese expatriate population organize Japanese businessmen's clubs such as Japanese chambers of commerce, golf clubs, tennis clubs, Mah-Jongg clubs, and other social clubs among themselves. They hold golf tournaments, tennis matches, and dinner parties attended only by Japanese businessmen and their family members. The wives get together among themselves for various social activities and maintain little contact with local residents. In addition, it is not unusual to find Japanese companies concentrated in a few downtown office buildings, and Japanese restaurants and karaoke bars that cater exclusively to Japanese businessmen in the nearby business districts. In other words, the Japanese families living in the same locality form a "little Tokyo" and continue to live as if they were in Japan. For these reasons the Japanese have acquired a bad reputation for being "clannish."

To alleviate this cliquishness of the Japanese expatriates, some Japanese multinationals sponsor Japanese-style company-wide social events at their overseas subsidiaries to promote good-will and friendship between the Japanese management and the local managers and employees. These events include annual company picnics, Christmas parties, golf tournaments, and anniversary dinners paid for by the company. The coordinators for these events try to facilitate informal contacts among those who are attending so that they can get to know each other personally.

166

Language and Cultural Barriers to Communication

As it was mentioned earlier, almost all Japanese multinationals have company-sponsored English classes or give financial assistance to those employees who wish to study English or other foreign languages. Those who are to be assigned to overseas subsidiaries are usually given several weeks of intensive English lessons before departure. However, the average Japanese businessman does not have a good command of English. He may have a thick Japanese accent, and it may even be difficult to understand what he is saying. Even if he speaks some English, he is likely not to comprehend spoken English very well. He may find it difficult to understand English spoken at a normal speed. Obviously, this is a critical weakness in face-to-face communication. He might have been sent abroad on the erroneous assumption that anybody can learn English (or any other language) within several months if he is thrown into a foreign environment. The irony of this situation is that his poor command of English not only makes interpersonal communication extremely difficult, but also makes his subordinates doubt his effectiveness as a manager.

In English-speaking countries such as the United States, Canada, England, Australia, and New Zealand, where speaking good English means a high level of acculturation and proper education, people with thick foreign accents are often looked down upon as poorly educated or new immigrants. Although these overseas Japanese businessmen are neither poorly educated nor new immigrants, they are not totally free from this stigma no matter how slight their foreign accent may be. English-speaking subordinates may show disrespect toward Japanese managers who speak "funny English." They may even poke fun at their managers' mispronunciation, improper accents, or poor grammar behind their backs when they feel unjustly reprimanded. To make matters worse, almost all Japanese managers are apprehensive and apologetic about their poor English and even doubt their ability to communicate in English. Some of them may try to cover up the feelings of inadequacy by "proudly" speaking broken English. Their attitude can be, "If you don't understand my English, you study Japanese."

Many of the Japanese managers are therefore compelled to depend upon their bilingual secretary or staff assistant to interpret and translate their oral instructions and written messages. This heavy dependence on the bilingual staff tends to reduce the managers' effectiveness, for such dependence is an open admission that they are deficient in communication competency, which is one of the most important managerial skills. This need for dependence on the bilingual staff may also disrupt the organizational hierarchy because the Japanese-speaking assistants can become too important to the managers' survival. In turn, this can create hard feelings or even jealousy among those local managers and employees who cannot speak Japanese.

A simple way to overcome this linguistic barrier is to assign only English-speaking managers and supervisors to overseas positions. However, it is not an easy task for many Japanese multinationals, especially for those smaller subcontractors, to find enough employees who have both technical competence and adequate language facility. Even though every Japanese businessman has studied English for at least ten years before he graduated from college and continued to study after graduation, he may not be well-trained in spoken English. The insularity of Japanese society also makes it difficult for them to practice English with native speakers. Most Japanese businessmen have had few opportunities to speak English until assigned to their overseas posts. Besides, they feel awkwardness or *iwakan* (a sense of incompatibility) when

167

meeting foreigners. March claims that the Japanese still have a *gai-jin* (foreigner) complex against English-speaking Caucasians, whom they consider (often reluctantly) more advanced, wealthier, more cosmopolitan, more self-assured, better-proportioned, better-looking, and more sexually attractive.[8] Consequently, they tend to be shy and hesitate to speak English even though their English may be quite good.

An apparent solution to this problem would be for Japanese multinationals to hire young Japanese men and women who have been educated in the English-speaking countries in the West. However, these Western-educated and competent Japanese individuals are not necessarily welcomed by most Japanese multinationals. They are considered "too Westernized" and no longer "real Japanese" in thought and action. Japanese corporations still prefer to hire new graduates directly from prestigious Japanese universities and then indoctrinate them into their respective corporate cultures. They fear that hiring Westernized recruits might disrupt the traditional work culture and the nature of interpersonal relationships within the organization. In some instances, having bilingual ability and bicultural knowledge can become a liability instead of an asset in tradition-bound and ethnocentric Japanese business organizations.

This language barrier creates still another problem for non-Japanese-speaking local managers who frequently need to communicate with Japanese counterparts over important issues. When it comes to touchy issues, the Japanese suddenly start discussions in Japanese among themselves. When the non-Japanese-speaking side asks for interpretation, the Japanese managers may give them abbreviated or "edited" information only and say that they will explain the whole thing later. The local managers naturally suspect that the Japanese managers are keeping secrets from them by intentionally speaking in Japanese. They might be correct in this assumption, but it is more likely that the Japanese do not want to use English when talking to each other unless all of them are equally competent and will feel comfortable in doing so. The only way for the local managers to find out what was actually talked about in Japanese is to ask one of the junior managers on the Japanese side who speaks good English to talk to them in private after the formal meeting over a cup of coffee or a few drinks.

Personnel Management Policy and Reward System

The Japanese style of personnel management and reward system will invariably become the source of frustrations for non-Japanese managers and employees working for Japanese multinationals. Most Japanese businesses still prefer to hire only Japanese nationals and Japanese expatriates already living overseas. If they need to recruit foreigners, they are more likely to hire descendants of Japanese immigrants and other Asians whose culture is similar to that of Japan. They give preferential treatment to male employees over female employees. The reward system is still based on seniority and group effort rather than on individual achievements. It goes without saying that this Japanese personnel management policy and reward system do not go well with those foreign employees whose culture is based on individualism and egalitarianism. In fact, many Japanese multinationals operating in the United States have been sued by their aggrieved employees and had to pay millions of dollars in actual and punitive damages; some have been forced to pay huge fines for violating the U.S. Equal Employment Opportunity Act.[9]

169

Japanese people's feelings toward foreigners seem to range from a mild sense of uneasiness to a strong dislike, depending on the nationality, ethnicity, culture, history, and economic power of the country the foreigners come from. Generally speaking, the Japanese have more positive feelings toward Caucasian Americans and Europeans, but they have a strong dislike toward racial minorities. They even hold a sense of superiority over other Asian neighbors such as Chinese and Koreans with whom they supposedly share the same ethnicity and a similar cultural heritage. These feelings held by the Japanese unfortunately have become the fundamental causes of discriminatory treatment of foreign managers and employees. Ordinarily, almost all foreign managers are hired as *shokutaku* or "nonregular staff" for a specified contract period, and non-Japanese employees are hired simply as just workers, without the privilege of lifetime employment. As explained before, the foreign managers will never be promoted to top positions with real responsibility and authority. They must be content with number two or number three positions no matter how long and how hard they might have worked for their Japanese employer. They should realize that they will be excluded from top management meetings unless they are fluent in Japanese and able to communicate with the Japanese expatriate managers without any difficulty. They may receive relatively good pay, but they will probably not be given the special allowances and generous entertainment expenses that their Japanese counterparts receive. Even if the regular employees do not have Japanese managers as their immediate superiors, they will be expected to abide by strict work rules and work diligently at all times. They also will be expected to work strictly as team members, not as individuals seeking to gain personal merit.

Sex Discrimination and Racial Discrimination in the Workplace

Because Japanese society has long been influenced by Confucian teachings on proper social relationships, Japanese women have for centuries played subordinate roles to men. Even after many decades of Westernization, Japan has not changed into an egalitarian society as yet. Despite the fact that the Equal Employment opportunity Act became effective on April 1, 1986, discrimination against women still seems to persist at workplaces in Japan. This law requires that employers "endeavor" to give equal opportunity and treatment to men and women, but there are no penalties levied against those employers that do not endeavor to follow the law.[10] Women are considered less dependable, less professional, and less capable. They also feel strong social pressures to play the traditional roles of *ryōsai kenbo* or "good wife, wise mother." Consequently, most working women are rarely given permanent positions with responsibilities no matter how well educated and how professionally competent they might be. This sex discrimination apparently exists in Japanese multinational companies operating in foreign countries as well.

In the United States, several Japanese multinational companies have been sued for sex discrimination, sexual harassment, and racial discrimination and have had to pay huge sums of money for actual and punitive damages. Nonetheless, few American women are recruited for responsible management positions with Japanese subsidiaries in the United States. They are usually hired as executive secretaries and administrative assistants to help their Japanese bosses in writing and editing letters, memos, and reports in English. They are also expected to do some domestic chores at the office such as serving coffee or tea, washing cups, running errands, and helping with nonwork-related personal matters. If doing these chores bothers American female employees of a Japanese firm, they should politely explain to their bosses that American executive secretaries and administrative assistants are not expected to perform these chores. They have important official duties to perform as professionals. However, they could volunteer to serve coffee or tea for important visitors if no other person can help with this chore. They could also volunteer to help the Japanese bosses in case of a family emergency or other situations where immediate assistance is necessary.

171

Sexual harassment has become a serious problem for Japanese multinational companies in the United States. Japanese men do not seem to know how to conduct themselves properly with young Western women. They have a different mind-set regarding sexual mores based on the Japanese concept of women.[11] The typical Japanese business entertainment includes drinking, dining, and sex. Many businessmen frequently go to hostess bars and places for male-only entertainment. Some of them are extremely curious about the bodies of Caucasian women and may have a sexual fantasy. The popular Hollywood depiction of sexually loose, fun-loving, blonde and blue-eyed women could have led them to believe that they can approach American women at work for sexual favors. Frequent company-sponsored socials and special dinners for overtime work or weekend work create many opportunities for Japanese managers to become friendly with their female secretaries and assistants. They may tell sex jokes and ask very personal questions about a woman's age, marriage, boyfriends, dress size, and leisure activity and even ask her to go out for dinner after work. When they get drunk, they may even "accidentally" touch the women close to them. A simple piece of advice is to draw the line from the beginning and not to tolerate any sexual harassment. If sexual harassment persists, it may become necessary to give the Japanese managers a copy of American laws regarding sexual harassment and help them understand the serious consequences of their seemingly innocent sexual advances. It is an excellent idea to help the company draw up a set of rules on personal conduct at the workplace; these should be published in both English and Japanese and distributed to every manager and employee in order to avoid costly lawsuits against sexual harassment and other misconduct.

Racial discrimination has also been a serious problem with overseas Japanese multinational companies. Several of these companies operating in the United States have been found liable for legal fees, fines, actual and punitive damages, and compensation to the aggrieved employees. The root of this problem can be traced to the historical fact that Japan had 250 years of seclusion imposed by the Tokugawa shogunate. During this period of seclusion, the Japanese developed an insular mentality, xenophobia, and ethnocentrism. Japan's geographic isolation and its prolonged process of cultural and racial homogenization led them to believe that they are a unique and superior people. From the Meiji period of 1868 to 1912 until the end of World War II in 1945, state Shintoism reinforced the superiority complex among the Japanese.[12] More recently, Japan's emergence as an economic superpower has reinforced the sense of superiority over other races. This superiority complex, in turn, becomes the root of discrimination toward certain ethnic groups based on their racial origins. Many Japanese have some prejudice against Europeans and white Americans, but they have much stronger prejudice against Arabs, Southeast Asians, and Africans. Consequently, it is difficult for the Japanese to accept members of other races as equals in many work-related situations. With a few exceptions, most of the Japanese multinational companies are staffed with East Asians whose physical features, culture and customs, and work ethics are considered similar to those of the Japanese. The Japanese generally feel uncomfortable and apprehensive working in truly multiracial and multicultural social settings. It has not been uncommon in the past to see a Japanese multinational company with top management positions occupied by the Japanese managers from Japan, lower-ranking positions staffed by local resident Japanese, Chinese, or Koreans. In some companies, there is a "token Caucasian," "token black," or "token Chicano" in a management position. Usually, these people are given such positions mainly to comply with local antidiscrimination laws and for public relations. Nevertheless, today many Japanese are making an earnest effort toward hiring non-Japanese as managers and supervisors because they are aware that changes need to be made to meet the increasing demand of making their overseas operations truly multinational. Despite such efforts, it may take a few more decades of internationalization of Japanese society before Japanese businesspeople can willingly accept and trust foreigners as dependable and trustworthy colleagues.

Employment Contract and Job Description

In Japan, the kind of employment contract found in Western countries, one with specific job descriptions, is very uncommon. For example, a *jirei* or "letter of appointment" simply says, "You will be assigned to the Marketing Department." The new employee will need to learn what he or she is expected to do by going through an orientation, classroom training sessions, and on the-job-training. Most overseas Japanese multinationals may have employment contracts patterned after the local business custom, but these contracts are often treated as mere formalities. In many instances, the contracts have implicit "unwritten segments" that should be understood and complied with without asking additional compensation. For example, an American senior manager's employment contract may call for a five-day workweek, but when a Japanese executive from the home office visits for an important meeting, the American manager may be required to show up for a meeting, even though it may be held on a Saturday afternoon. He may also be expected to play golf on Sunday and socialize with the Japanese guest.

Sometimes an employment contract may be arbitrarily canceled before its expiration. When this happens, the Japanese managers usually do not give specific reasons for cancellation with the excuse that doing so may hurt the feelings of the dismissed. They often use informal intermediaries, not lawyers, to persuade the employee to resign, as is the custom in Japan. In some instances, they may make up a seemingly legitimate excuse or even use an outright lie so apparent that the targeted employee can see the real reason for dismissal. For example, the Japanese personnel manager may say, "We will need to cut some positions because the company is having a serious financial difficulty," when in fact the business is going well. In other words, the official reason for dismissal must be made socially acceptable to avoid loss of face for the dismissed employee.

Lifetime employment is an attractive option for any employee. Many local people join overseas Japanese multinational companies with an expectation that the practice of lifetime employment will apply to them, too. It is true that some Japanese companies even promise overseas employees lifetime tenure. However, it is naive to assume that the Japanese company will keep this promise; instead, the company will adopt the local employment practices of hiring, layoffs, and dismissal when it becomes convenient to do so. The Japanese companies do not hesitate to apply the concept of *jijō henkō* or "doctrine of changed circumstance" to an employment contract.[13] This means that the contract can be modified or canceled if the circumstances have changed from the time of the initial contract. In other words, it is unwise to believe that an overseas Japanese multinational company would adhere to the unique employment system of Japan when doing business overseas.

Despite these drawbacks, overseas Japanese multinational companies are still good employers for aspiring non-Japanese workers who are willing to learn and adjust to Japanese corporate culture, unique interpersonal relationships, and different ways of doing business. The Japanese multinationals are definitely aware that the success of their overseas operations requires good managers, supervisors, and workers from the local communities in which they operate. A big challenge for non-Japanese people working under Japanese management is to take upon themselves the task of becoming a bicultural person and a "cultural bridge" between Japan and their own country.

174

chapter 9

Living and Working in Japan

Japan is a very Westernized country in Asia. The large metropolitan cities of Japan are just like those of the United States and other Western countries in appearance. Nevertheless, many decades of strong Western influence have not really changed the basic Japanese national characteristics. The government is bureaucratic; the immigration laws are strict; roads and highways are congested; living accommodations are expensive and different; home appliances and furniture are small; food habits are different; social customs and interpersonal relationships are uniquely Japanese; and businesses are run according to Japanese rules. Many foreigners coming to live and work in Japan, especially Westerners, naively assuming that it is a modern cosmopolitan country, are not well prepared to encounter the vast cultural differences they will have to face. They will undoubtedly experience severe culture shock, and they will need to make physical, mental, and psychological adjustments. Historically speaking, the Japanese have always had a negative attitude toward foreigners and looked at them with suspicion and distrust. To them, all foreigners are *gaijin*. They still frown upon interethnic marriages. Despite the rapid Americanization of Japanese society, the Japanese still cling to their old ways. They may drink Coca Cola, eat McDonald's hamburgers, enjoy Hollywood movies, go to Tokyo Disneyland, and play TV games, but they also drink green tea, eat raw fish, enjoy watching sumo matches, go to kabuki plays, and play Japanese chess games. Insights into various aspects of life in Japan and the unique characteristics of the Japanese people will be absolutely necessary for the foreigners residing in Japan.

The Attitude of Japanese Government Authorities

Despite the fact that the Japanese government has been maintaining diplomatic and trade relations with foreign countries, it has not changed the xenophobic attitude that came from the many international conflicts in its long history. Unlike the United States and some other Western countries, Japan does not give citizenship automatically to babies born in Japan of parents who are not Japanese citizens. It also imposes very strict rules on permanent resident status and even more stringent conditions for naturalization. Work visas are not easy to obtain. All applicants for work visas need to present a certificate of employment and a letter of guarantee from the employer in Japan. In addition, they need to have *hoshonin* or "guarantors" who are Japanese nationals with good professional and social standing to guarantee in writing their financial support and proper personal conduct. All foreigners who intend to spend at least three consecutive months in Japan must report to local government authorities and obtain a Certificate of Alien Registration within ninety days of arrival. Foreigners sixteen years of age and older are required to carry their Alien Registration Card at all times. Any foreigner who wishes to leave Japan temporarily will need to obtain a reentry permit regardless of the reasons for and duration of the stay outside the country. When the foreigner leaves Japan permanently, the Certificate of Alien Registration must be relinquished. Duration of the permitted stay varies depending on the type of visa, but the period of the stay stamped into the passport by the immigration officer legally overrides any prior recommendation written by a Japanese embassy or consular official overseas. The officer can deny entry to people suffering from epidemic illness and mental sickness, people likely to become public charges, exconvicts, narcotics users, prostitutes, deportees, terrorists, and other undesirables. If the foreigner wishes to extend his stay, he must begin the extension process by submitting the necessary documents long before the period of the stay authorized by the visa expires. It is important to know that visa status cannot be changed after one arrives in Japan. The applicant must leave Japan while waiting for a new visa. It is possible, however, to go to a nearby foreign country where Japanese consular service is available and apply for the visa status change. For example, an American English teacher who entered Japan as a tourist will not be allowed to stay on in Japan and apply for a work visa. But he or she may go to Korea or Hong Kong to apply for it and reenter Japan once the work visa is granted.

Japanese government officials, sensitive to signs of disrespect, encroachment, and falsehood, often give the impression that they are cold, unfriendly, and arrogant. They have traditionally been authoritarian and formal when they are on official duty and in uniform. Clearly, they are not members of a Japanese government welcoming committee. They are inspectors whose official duty is to protect their country from undesirable foreigners. It is always wise to deal with them with politeness, humility, and respect, even though some of them may have limited competence in English. Demanding prompt attention or special attention may antagonize them. Likewise, overly friendly verbal or nonverbal behaviors toward them may arouse suspicion. Never argue with them under any circumstance, and be quick to apologize if something goes wrong. Unlike the situation in some Asian countries, a bribe is never openly accepted in Japan. If one needs a special favor from a Japanese government official, an arrangement must be worked out in strict privacy through a "proper channel."

Transportation Systems in Japan

Japan has developed the world's best mass transit system because it has always needed efficient transportation to carry millions of passengers and millions of tons of cargo throughout the country. Japan has the world's most efficient passenger train system of *shinkansen* or "bullet-train" networks run by Japan Railways (JR) and domestic airline operations. In metropolitan areas, there are convenient subways and monorails. In addition, buses, minibuses, and taxis provide additional means of transportation. Even with all these convenient modes of transportation, foreigners can get into trouble unless they learn how to use them.

The bullet-train system is the most convenient means of ground transportation for long-distance travel. Frequent bullet-train services carry millions of passengers between major cities. For example, for the Tokyo-Kyoto-Nagoya-Osaka sector, the bullet trains run at five-minute intervals during peak hours. They stop for about thirty or forty seconds at each stop for passenger loading and unloading. Passengers need to be alert and prepared to get off or get on very quickly. All trains have three classes of service: green car or reserved first class *(gurinsha)*, reserved *(shiteiseki)*, and unreserved *(jiyūseki)*. They are also divided into nonsmoking cars *(kinensha)* and smoking cars *(kitsuensha)*. The green cars are all reserved and very comfortable, and soft drinks, hot or cold towels, and reading materials are provided, but the ticket is very expensive.

The Japan Railway system offers an excursion pass called "Japan Railway Pass" that is available only to foreigners visiting Japan on holiday. This pass must be purchased overseas and exchanged for coupons at designated places upon arrival in Japan. It provides a substantial discount and convenience for traveling over many sectors of the Japan Railway system during the specified period of time of one week, two weeks, or three weeks. It is advisable to make seat reservations and buy the tickets in advance and to go to the correct train platform at least ten minutes early.

Domestic airline links are also very extensive, and frequent scheduled services are available to almost all cities in Japan. The three major carriers—Japan Air Lines, All Nippon Airways, and Japan Air System—monopolize airline services within Japan. Foreign airlines are not allowed to fly between domestic destinations. Foreign visitors who fly into Japan on non-Japanese airlines cannot fly to another domestic destination within Japan except in transit to a foreign destination. Since Japan is a small country, most flights are one or two hours and are run much like commuter airlines in the United States and Europe. Daily television news provides information on schedules and seat availability for viewers' convenience. The airlines now sell flight coupons and tickets from many convenience stores in big cities. Consequently, air travel is becoming a common means of transportation.

Taking subways is a very convenient and efficient way to travel in big cities. The road traffic is so heavy, especially during peak commuting hours, that it becomes impossible to travel by a private car or taxi. For example, there are extensive networks of twelve different subway lines in the Tokyo metropolitan area for the convenience of millions of commuters coming from the surrounding cities. These lines are color coded for easy identification, and each train stop has the station name in both Japanese characters and *rōmaji* (English characters). There are many vending machines for ticket purchases (also color coded) for the convenience of passengers. The subway lines also sell train passes for a certain number of rides.

Electric trains also serve short and long distances and are another convenient and dependable means of transportation. Just like subways, these trains are color coded according to the types of service. The train services are categorized into superexpress *(tokkyū)*, semisuper express *(junkyū)*, express *(kyūko)*, and local *(kakueki)*. A serious problem for foreigners who do not speak Japanese is to know which type of train to take. In some cases, trains that leave from the same platform do not stop at all the same stations along the way. It is always wise to read the destination sign or ask the train staff on duty which train to take. Foreigners who get lost should not ask a passerby for help, but go to the Information Desk. Japanese people are generally very shy and rather cold to strangers.

A caution must be given to those foreigners who need to travel during morning and evening rush hours in big cities. The commuter trains are tightly packed. No priority is given to women or senior citizens during rush hours. Young women (especially young Caucasian women) bitterly complain about the "wandering hands" of some weird Japanese men in congested trains. On rainy days, wet umbrellas and wet clothing make it very unpleasant to ride the congested trains. Sometimes, the last commuter trains leaving the city centers at midnight have drunks who misbehave and act foolishly in public. The stereotypical image of Japanese being polite and humble does not apply in these situations.

Intercity buses have become a popular means of transportation for the young and the thrifty. These buses travel during the late night and early morning hours when highway traffic is not

179

heavy. For example, an intercity bus between Tokyo and Osaka leaves late at night and arrives in the early morning of the following day.

City buses provide short trips with many stops for local residents and commuters. The fare is paid in advance or at the time of exit into the fare box. Sometimes it is difficult to see how much fare to pay unless the passenger can read the destinations written in *kanji* and is familiar with the locality.

Other buses are for sightseeing and excursion trips for group travel. These buses are very popular with schools and with business and civic organizations because they are equipped with karaoke equipment and a small refrigerator. Students on school excursions and tourists on group tours ride these buses to tourist destinations and enjoy themselves.

All Japanese taxis have meters standardized by the local government; fares are based on kilometers driven and time spent waiting in heavy traffic. Other charges added to the metered fares are highway toll charges and "midnight extra charges" of 30 percent for taxi rides between 11:00 P.M. and 5:00 A.M. The taxis are of two kinds: *kojin takushī* (operated by the owner-driver) and *kaisha takushī* (company owned and operated). The former is often cleaner and provides more courteous service, because the driver himself is the owner. *Kaisha takushī* drivers are hired on fixed pay plus commission, but they are well-trained and provide the proper service required by the company they work for. Nowadays there is a new type of taxi called *wagonsha* (station wagon taxi) for passengers who have a lot of baggage. Ordinary Japanese taxis do not have enough trunk space. Almost all taxis in Japan use liquid natural gas (propane) for fuel and have a huge gas storage tank in the trunk. The left back door of all Japanese taxis is opened and closed automatically with a lever by the driver.

Another form of automobile transportation is *haiyā* (hire), a larger, cleaner, deluxe Japanese or foreign car with a chauffeur. The fare for this service is either a fixed fee for point-to-point service or is based on time spent driving and waiting. Although *haiyā* provides a much more comfortable ride and very courteous service, it is used only by top business executives and high-ranking politicians because it is far more expensive than a taxi ride. Before using a taxi or a chauffeured car, it is wise to find out in advance the approximate fare to the destination. For example, the taxi fare from Tokyo International Airport to downtown Tokyo is about $200, and the hire charge is more than $400. International passengers are advised to take either a limousine bus or airport express trains whose fare is about $30 or $40. To avoid paying too much for ground transportation, it is wise to check the in-flight magazine for airport-city transfer fares, schedules, and travel time. It is also advisable to carry a bilingual map of the area with the destinations written in Japanese and to have the building name and other landmarks in addition to the address. Most Japanese taxi drivers do not understand English, and they will be frustrated and may become discourteous if they cannot understand the instructions.

Driving a private car in Japan is not only expensive but also requires coping with other inconveniences. Before running out to buy a car in Japan, it is important to consider many factors such as driving conditions, insurance, parking, and traffic regulations. A booklet, *Rules of the Road*, published by the Japan Automobile Association will answer many questions. First of all, a foreign driver's license is not valid for driving in Japan. Application for a Japanese license is made at the license office nearest to one's residence. The minimum age for obtaining the license is eighteen. It is relatively easy to obtain if the applicant has a valid foreign driver's license. If not, he or she is required to take two written tests in English and two driving tests. Japanese people usually attend driver-training schools to prepare for these tests. An American-made car with its steering wheel on the left side is inconvenient and even dangerous to use in Japan because the Japanese drive on the left side of the road. All Japanese cars are made for the Japanese market and have the steering wheel on the right-hand side of the car.

Parking is always a problem in Japan because parking spaces are not only very small but also expensive to rent. The Japanese law requires that a car buyer show written proof certified by the local police that he or she has an off-street parking space. Condominium apartments do not usually provide free parking spaces even for residents; they generally pay $300–$500 a month for a parking space.

City streets are extremely narrow with no sidewalks, and the main streets are crowded with many minitrucks, motorcycles, scooters, bicycles, and pedestrians. Today Japan uses international traffic signs, but there are few English signs, and street addresses are too small to see. Penalties for traffic violations and drunken driving

181

are very severe: punishment includes imprisonment, stiff fines, or suspension of one's driver's license.

Hotels and Living Accommodations

Japan is the most developed country in Asia, and big cities like Tokyo, Yokohama, Kyoto, Nagoya, Osaka, and Kobe have many excellent Western-style hotels, condominium apartments, and houses suitable for Westerners. There is a wide range of hotels: deluxe Western-style hotels, business hotels, motels, and Japanese inns *(ryokan)*. All of these hotels are required to maintain certain standards of physical facilities and services designated by the Japanese government. Western-style condominium apartments and houses are also available in the city and in the suburbs. However, these accommodations are very expensive because real estate prices in Japan are prohibitively high, especially in central urban areas.

Good hotels in Japan compare favorably with first-class hotels in the United States and Europe. These hotels have spacious, clean rooms and provide guests with many amenities such as English-language TV channels, English newspapers, tea and coffee, a minibar, bathrobes, toiletries, and slippers. Many of the deluxe hotels have a health spa, beauty salon, tennis courts, swimming pool, and even a business center, but room rates are very high, and guests have to pay extra for every service. Meals at hotel restaurants are very expensive, and a 10 percent consumption tax and 10 percent service charge are added to the bills automatically.

There are Western-style business hotels whose rates are reasonable, but rooms are very small, and only minimum services are available. For tall and big Westerners, the rooms may be too small and the beds too short and narrow. The business hotels usually have coffee-shop type restaurants and snack bars for simple meals and drinks as well as vending machines that dispense cold canned beer, soft drinks, snacks, and toiletry items.

Motels in Japan are not the same as those found in the United States and Europe. Rather, they are "love hotels" where couples can spend a few hours together or have an overnight stay. They are usually near the highway exits and busy city districts with nightclubs and hostess bars and are not suitable for motorists who want regular accommodations.

Japanese inns are quite different from Western-style hotels in accommodations and meal service. The rooms do not have beds. Instead, futons or large Japanese cushions are placed on the floor for sleeping. Futons are stored in the room's closet and are taken out at bedtime and put back in the morning by the room maid. Dinners are usually served in the room, although some Japanese inns serve all meals in a large dining room. Although guests can enjoy courteous Japanese-style service in such inns, there are a few disadvantages and inconveniences. One thing that usually bothers Westerners is that there is little privacy. It is like living in a small house with a butler and a maid who try to attend to your every need. Another thing is the use of a large community bath or *ōburo*, which is used by all the guests. Although there are separate baths for men and women, many Westerners hesitate going naked among the curious Japanese guests. Some deluxe rooms have a small bath in the room, but the major attraction of Japanese inns is the large community bath in which the guests can leisurely take a long bath. Most of these Japanese inns are in hot spring resorts where they can use abundant hot spring water containing medicinal minerals. Before getting into the big bath, the bathers must wash themselves clean in the washing area, equipped with showerheads; they also take a shower again after having soaked themselves for a while. Nudity in this situation is considered completely normal in Japan.

Japanese inns charge their guests on a per person, not a per room basis; the price includes dinner and breakfast. If the charge for one night is, say, $300, the charge for four people would be $1,200 even if they occupy the same room. Meals are Japanese-style with raw fish, grilled fish, cooked meats and vegetables, pickles, seaweed, tofu (fermented soybean curd), rice, and miso soup. Some of these food items may not look palatable to Westerners, but they are quite tasty once one gets used to eating them.

Western-style houses and condominium apartments *(man-shon)* are available for rent, but they are smaller and cost a lot more than those in the West. These are for *gaijin* only; ordinary Japanese families cannot afford to live in them. For example, a condominium or a house adequate for a family of four in a central location in Tokyo would cost $15,000 to $30,000 a month. In addition, tenants need to pay an initial lump-sum payment that includes an advance payment of rent of three months, *shikikin* (non-interest-bearing deposit) of three months' rent, *reikin* (monetary gift) to the landlord of three months' rent, and a real estate agent fee equivalent to one month's rent. All of these payments add up to a total of ten months' rent if the agent's fee is included. The deposit is usually refunded at the end of the rental contract minus fees for damages, but some landlords do not make any refund unless the premises are "like new" when vacated. Maintaining a large Western-style condominium or a house with air-conditioning and heating units would be very expensive because utility charges are quite high and all the utilities including water are paid by the tenants. To solve this difficult housing problem, most foreign businesses and other organizations usually provide housing for expatriate staff and their families in Japan. They either buy housing units or have long-term leases with the landlords and sublet them to their staff members. Japanese companies hiring employees from foreign countries usually provide subsidized housing because it is almost impossible for the foreign staff to rent an apartment or house on their own.

College students living in Japan usually stay at a student dormitory or *geshuku* (rooming house for students). A *geshuku* is often operated as a family business, and the proprietor provides a small room with a desk, meals, and sometimes laundry service. Toilet facilities are usually shared. Many foreign students are encouraged to choose homestay with Japanese families, but they should not expect to enjoy privacy and personal freedom. Native speakers of English can teach English to the children of host families and earn some income. In all cases of housing or room rental, it is necessary to have a reputable Japanese individual or employer vouch in writing for timely payment of rent and take full responsibility for any damages or complaints.

It is also important to know in advance that Japanese home appliances such as water heaters, refrigerators, and bathtubs are much smaller than those found in Western homes. Furniture can also be smaller unless it is imported from Western countries. Americans used to having large home appliances and furniture may have difficulty in making adjustments. They will find the regular Japanese refrigerator very inconvenient as it is just too small for all the food and beverages that they want to store. And because electric current in Japan is 60 cycles and 100 volts, appliances made in other countries will need transformers.

Shopping and Dining

Shopping and dining in Japan can be a lot of fun, although things are getting expensive because the Japanese yen has gained value against other world currencies in recent years. There are many large department stores, discount stores, supermarkets, and specialty shops where shoppers can buy a wide variety of Japanese-made products as well as imported luxury merchandise from all over the world.

Department stores in big cities are a delightful place to go shopping because they offer not only a huge variety of merchandise but also have many restaurants, coffee shops, and special exhibitions to delight shoppers. These department stores carry brand-name merchandise of all kinds and usually include a cosmetics sales floor, jewelry department, and toy department; in addition, they also include specialty stores and supermarket sections with fresh fruits, vegetables, fish, meats, and cakes and pastries; usually there is a small amusement park on the top floor. Shoppers can literally spend hours at such department stores. Unlike in other Asian countries, bargaining is not practiced in these stores although it may be done in small stores on the streets. In addition to department stores, there are discount stores for electronics, cameras, and video recorders. Bargain hunting can be fun if the shoppers know what they are buying. Supermarkets have all sorts of food items that are neatly arranged. Because meat, fresh fish, and fruits of good quality are very expensive, these items are sold by 100 grams (3.5 ounces), not by pounds or kilograms. Neighborhood specialty shops are good places to buy things because they provide personalized service to regular customers including free delivery service.

Dining in Japan is very enjoyable. The vast number of restaurants offers a large variety of culinary experiences. There are tens of thousands of restaurants in the big cities that serve everything from authentic French cuisine to Japanese delicacies. Invasions of American fast-food chains like McDonald's, Kentucky Fried Chicken, Domino's Pizza, Sizzler Steakhouse, Red Lobster, and Dunkin' Donuts gives an appearance that the Japanese have adopted all of these American foods, but they also eat many different kinds of foods including Southeast Asian, Middle Eastern, European, Russian, and Polynesian. Foreign residents should learn to enjoy varieties of unique Japanese cuisine in addition to those

185

well-known and already popular Japanese dishes in many parts of the world.

Types of restaurants range from those serving top-class Japanese cuisine to informal sushi bars and boisterous neighborhood eating and drinking places. All of these restaurants are licensed by the local government and follow its strict health and hygienic standards. It is quite safe to eat and drink at these establishments. Such dishes as *tempura*, *yakitori*, *sukiyaki*, *shabu shabu*, and *teppan yaki* are appreciated by almost everyone, but for other Japanese delicacies, the taste may need to be acquired by trying them a few times. *Sashimi* is fresh raw fish filleted into small slices and attractively arranged on a dish with shredded *daikon* (Japanese radish), a bit of sliced cucumber, carrots, and seaweed. There are many types of *sashimi*, but the most popular ones are slices of yellow-fin tuna *(maguro)*, bonito *(katsuo)*, salmon *(shake)*, flounder *(hirame)*, sea bream *(tai)*, scallops *(kaibashira)*, octopus *(tako)*, and cuttlefish *(ika)*. Some other unique raw seafood dishes are *ikezukuri* (a whole live fish sliced up), *odori* ("jumping" shrimps), and sea urchin *(uni)*. These dishes may sound unappetizing and even cruel to Westerners, but they are real delicacies for the Japanese. Other, more-exotic dishes are broiled eels *(unagi)* served with a sweet, delicious soy sauce, and puffer fish *(fugu)* served as *sashimi* or in a tasty broth with vegetables. Eating this puffer fish may require some courage, because it has a poisonous liver and ovaries. Chefs preparing it must be trained and licensed by the local chefs' association to eliminate any chance of poisoning by improper preparation.

The existence of all these "weird Japanese foods" does not mean that the foreign residents must force themselves to eat them. There are many other palatable dishes to choose from among other Japanese foods. For customers' convenience, most restaurants either offer menus with color pictures of popular dishes or show quite realistic plastic models of items in the show windows. For those who do not want to cook but have meals at home, neighborhood restaurants provide *demae* (delivery service). In fact, customers can order a wide variety of dishes cooked fresh from a nearby restaurant and have them delivered to their homes within twenty or thirty minutes. Japanese housewives keep a list of restaurants that provide this service so that they can order good dishes for unexpected guests on short notice. This is similar to the delivery service of Domino's Pizza restaurants found in many countries except that these Japanese restaurants can deliver a complete lunch or dinner for a party of several people.

Socializing with Japanese Friends and Neighbors

The Japanese are generally not very sociable with foreigners. Even today the majority of Japanese have not had the experience of meeting and talking with people from other countries. They are reluctant to strike up a conversation with strangers unless they are properly introduced by mutual friends or acquaintances. The general attitude toward foreigners is ambivalent and even negative at times. All foreigners are categorized as *gaijin*, and all Caucasians are called *hakujin* (white people) regardless of nationality. Koreans and Chinese are called *daisangokujin* (third-country people).

Japanese make a clear distinction in associating with these different kinds of outsiders. They generally treat *hakujin* (especially Americans and British) better than other races. Immigrant workers from Iran, China, the Philippines, Malaysia, and South American countries are looked down upon because they are hired to do menial jobs that Japanese workers are unwilling to do. Their jobs are called "3-K jobs"—*kiken* (dangerous), *kitanai* (dirty), and *kitsui* (strenuous). These immigrants are often discriminated against both at work and in social situations. They may have difficulty in renting an apartment or may be treated unfairly at stores and local government offices.

Even in this rather unpleasant social climate, it would be wise for all foreign residents in Japan to try to socialize with Japanese neighbors and make new friends. However, they must learn Japanese social customs and proper protocol before jumping into establishing interpersonal contact with them. Foreigners need to learn different forms of greeting, social manners, and gift-giving customs.

Japanese is a highly status-oriented language, and it has several different level of politeness. Lower-status people speak politely to higher-status people. Women are expected to use more polite forms of speech than men. A simple greeting such as "Good morning" can be said in at least three different ways—*Ohayō goza-imasu*, *Ohayō*, and *Ohayo*—and choosing a wrong form of greeting can become a cause of embarrassment. When greeting the land-lord, it is proper to say *Ohayō gozaimasu*; to a friend, *Ohayō*; and *Ohayo* to a delivery man. Even though a minor mistake made by foreigners is usually tolerated, it is better to know how to say sim-ple greetings properly.

Americans living in Japan are often surprised that the Japanese never smile at them even when they happen to catch each other's eyes in an elevator or on the street. In the United States it is quite common to smile or even say "hello" just to be friendly, but in Japan people ignore the presence of strangers. From early childhood Japanese children are taught not to talk to strangers, and many of them tend to have *taijin kyōfu shō* or "phobia of interper-sonal relations."[1] It may seem that the Japanese are unsociable and unfriendly, but they can turn into sociable and friendly individuals if they meet new friends through a proper introduction and in proper social context. For example, the Japanese residents of a high-class condominium complex will welcome a new American family if the resident manager properly introduces them. Or an American woman can meet and make friends with Japanese women in the same cooking class offered by the Western food sales section of a department store. The Japanese need to know who and what newcomers are before they become friendly and sociable. This is why the Japanese ask the kinds of personal questions that Westerners may consider an invasion of personal privacy: "How old are you?" "Where were you born?" "What university did you or your husband (wife) graduate from?" "How much money does your husband make?" "How much did you pay for your nice hand-bag?" "Where are you going today?" The Japanese do not neces-sarily expect truthful answers to all such questions so Westerners can be evasive. For example, Westerners who do not want to answer a question about their age could reply, "I'm not too young, but old enough to have a ten-year old daughter." To the question on salary they could say, "I wish he made a lot more. Japan is a very expensive country to live in." The annoying "Where are you going today?" can be answered, "Oh, just down the street." Ambiguity and white lies are acceptable forms of denial in Japan. They should never flatly refuse to answer or show annoyance nonverbally no matter how meddlesome the questions may sound.

The Japanese are also quick to give compliments on a foreigner's Japanese-language ability and what he or she is wearing. The compliments, called *oseiji* or "social compliments," are a form of ritualistic communication. The Japanese compliment each other frequently, but they do not really mean what they are saying. For example, almost all Japanese say to a foreigner who speaks a little broken Japanese, "You speak good Japanese." The foreigner might be tempted to say, "Oh, thank you. I have worked hard on my Japanese." This innocent answer is a violation of social etiquette because it does not show humility. The foreigner should say, "Oh, but my Japanese is still very poor." A Western woman should answer a compliment on her new dress such as "What a beautiful dress you are wearing! It must have been very expensive" with a response like, "Oh, don't mention it. It wasn't expensive." She should never say, "Oh, thank you. You think it looks good on me? It cost me a bundle!"

Among the other important social manners are the following:

1. Do not call loudly and wave to people walking at a distance.

2. Do not call a person of higher status by his or her first name.

3. Do not act too friendly, and refrain from slapping or touching others on the back.

4. Do not shake hands indiscriminately; bow instead when it is more appropriate to do so.

5. Do not maintain direct eye contact for a long time during conversation.

6. Do not talk loudly in a crowd.

7. Do not cross your legs when talking to a superior.

8. Do not put your feet up on a desk or another piece of furniture and show the soles of your shoes.

9. Do not wear shoes into a Japanese house.

10. Do not blow your nose with a handkerchief and then put it back into your pocket; use facial tissue instead.

11. Do not point a finger at another person.

12. Do not hug or kiss Japanese friends in public even for friendly greetings.

13. Do not kiss babies or touch young children to show affection.

14. Do not dress too casually and wear loud-colored shirts or dresses unbecoming to your age or social status.

15. Do not eat when walking around.

16. Do not smile and greet perfect strangers with a casual "Hello."

Understanding the unique custom of gift giving is very important in socializing with the Japanese. There are two major gift-giving occasions in Japan: *Ochūgen* (midsummer gifts) are exchanged around the midsummer Buddhist festival of Obon in July; *Oseibo* (year-end gifts) are given at the end of December. Businesses give gifts to their client companies or individuals to thank them for their patronage. Relatives, friends, and neighbors also exchange gifts on these two occasions. Large department stores offer a huge variety of gift items during these gift-giving seasons and provide gift-wrapping and delivery service. The gifts are not usually given in person, but sent via *takkyubin* or "home delivery service." This is indeed a convenient service, because the givers do not have to carry around their gifts and personally deliver them to each of the receivers. It also provides secrecy when giving a gift to someone working for a company, government office, or educational institution. For example, a salesman can go to a department store and pick an expensive gift, then have it sent to the home of the purchasing manager of his client company via *takkyubin*, and others in the company will not know about this gift.

In addition, gifts are given on other occasions such as birthdays, matriculations, graduations, weddings, and the like. Condolence gifts (money or flowers or both) are given for funerals, and sympathy gifts for illness, hospitalization, fire, and other disasters. Visiting a relative or friend also requires a small gift called *temiyage*, which is a basket of fruit, a box of cookies, a can of green tea, or a bottle of sake or whiskey. It is a social infraction not to bring along a gift even when going only for tea or lunch.

A new family moving into a neighborhood should call on the neighbors with a small gift and introduce themselves and ask for assistance in person. When doing this, it is good to ask the landlord or the resident manager to come along because he or she can give a proper introduction to the neighbors. There are a few important social customs to remember in this social context: (1) A gift ought to be wrapped neatly with proper paper and presented with both hands. (2) The gift is not usually opened in front of the giver.[2] If it is a food item, it is not eaten then and there. (3) *Okaeshi* or "return gifts" are often given when the visitor is leaving. If the receiver does not have anything to return, a proper gift should be ordered and delivered from a reputable department store within a few days. Ideally it is at least slightly greater in value and quality than the gift received.

Japanese people always give gifts when they are asking for a favor, and they give another gift when the favor is done. If it is necessary to refuse doing a favor, the receiver of the gift can reciprocate it with a different gift of equal value. It is extremely impolite to flatly refuse to accept a gift or to return the same gift, even if the gift was given with an ulterior motive.

Education for Foreign Residents

Unlike English-speaking countries such as the United States, Britain, Canada, and Australia, Japan does not have a long history of educating foreigners in its schools. Only a small number of foreign students came to study in Japan before the 1970s, when it emerged as an economic superpower in Asia. Besides the difficulty of mastering the language, Japanese society has never been open to foreigners. Until recently, foreign students have had no choice but to attend American or Canadian international schools that are not accredited by the Japanese Ministry of Education. Today, because of the influx of foreign businesspeople, diplomats, and workers, many international schools and some Japanese schools have opened their doors to foreign residents. There are about twenty-five schools that offer educational programs in English from nursery to secondary level. Of these, thirteen are in the Tokyo and Yokohama area; the others are in Sapporo, Sendai, Nagoya, Kyoto, Nara, Osaka, Kobe, Hiroshima, Fukuoka, and Okinawa. In addition, there are French, German, Indonesian, Chinese, and Korean schools in Tokyo, and German and Norwegian schools in Kobe. At the university level, there are many colleges that offer "international programs" with instruction in English. At the trade-school level, there are Japanese language schools; martial art schools teaching subjects such as judo, kendo, and aikido; and cultural schools teaching subjects such as ikebana, tea ceremony *(sado)*, and traditional dancing and music. The following information will be helpful in understanding how these schools, universities, and other educational institutions are operated.

Many of the international schools in Japan are former mission schools established in the late nineteenth century for the purpose of spreading Christianity among the young Japanese, but today these schools are secularized and accept non-Christian students. Other international schools have been established by educational foundations in affiliation with American, British, or Canadian educational institutions for the express purpose of providing education for foreign residents in Japan. Some of the most famous Catholic schools are Saint Mary International School and St. Joseph International School in Yokohama, and International School of the Sacred Heart, Seisin International School, and Saint Maur International School in Tokyo. Other famous nonsectarian schools are the American School in Japan, the British School in Tokyo, the Canadian Academy in Kobe, and the Yokohama International School. These schools provide bilingual and multicultural education from preschool level to sixth grade, ninth grade or twelfth grade, with instruction given mainly in English.[3] Admission to these schools is very competitive; there are only a limited number of vacancies, and both foreign students and Japanese returnees *(kikokushijo)*★ compete for them. Tuition and fees are very high because many of the faculty members of these schools are hired from overseas and receive high wages and because land for school buildings is very expensive in Japan. Admission standards vary, but applicants are selected based on their proficiency in English, previous educational records, and placement test results.

For college-level education, there are a few branch campuses of foreign universities in Japan that cater to both foreign and Japanese students. Temple University has a branch in Tokyo, Minnesota State University in Niigata, and Michigan University in Otsu. In addition, there are *kokusaibu* or "international divisions" of well-established Japanese universities where foreign students can study their subjects in English. The most well known of these programs are the international division of Sophia University, International Christian University, Waseda University, Keio University in Tokyo, Nanzan University in Nagoya, Kansai Gaidai University in Osaka, and International University of Japan in Niigata. Recently some American universities have begun offering extension courses in business administration. These schools would be better suited for foreign students who do not have a good command of Japanese. To reach the competency in Japanese required for college-level work would take several years for those who do not have any background in Japanese. Students who take the international programs offered by these universities have the advantage of (1) learning about Japan in the actual cultural context of Japan; (2) studying and socializing with students from other foreign countries; and (3) transferring credits to institutions back home. Admission can be relatively easy for good students with high motivation, and many scholarships are also available through the Japan Foundation and other sources.

For those who wish to study the Japanese language or other subjects in Japanese martial arts, music, and art and culture, there are many choices of trade schools *(senmon gakkō)*. Admission

★ *"Kikokushijo"* refers to those Japanese students who were educated in English at overseas schools when their parents were on a foreign assignment. They prefer to attend international schools over Japanese schools because they are usually not good in Japanese and have acquired Western manners.

to these schools is much easier than to college or university programs. Anyone who can pay the tuition and fees will be admitted. Foreign students who wish to pursue careers in teaching Japanese martial arts or traditional Japanese music, arts, and art and culture can take courses in the subjects of their choice. These students usually have had years of training back home at branch schools and are invited to the headquarters in Japan for advanced study. These schools are also licensed by the local government, and offer apprenticeships and intensive training. Finally, many Japanese language schools have recently sprung up in several big cities for those foreigners who come to study Japanese and work part-time. The Japanese government allows foreigners to work twenty hours a week if they attend a licensed Japanese language school.

Finding Jobs in Japan

Despite Japan's continuing economic recession since 1991, Japanese companies and educational institutions are still hiring foreigners for various positions. There are four major job categories: business professionals, laborers, sports stars, and English teachers. Recruitment of foreign staff members and workers is usually conducted through overseas representatives or employment agencies. In almost all cases, such employment is on a *shokutaku* (contractual) basis for a fixed period of time and not on a permanent employment basis. The initial contract is usually for one year, and it is automatically renewed if the employer chooses to do so. A typical Japanese-style employment contract is a simple one: it stipulates only key clauses without specific job descriptions. Today many Japanese employers have begun to use an American-style contract with detailed employment conditions and job descriptions, but they often interpret and implement the contract in a somewhat Japanese way when it is convenient to do so. In many instances, when unexpected changes occur in economic conditions or other situations, Japanese employers do not hesitate to change the contractual terms with little regard to the sanctity of a written legal contract.[4] Japanese employers often expect that employees will be willing to do more than what the contract calls for if any additional work needs to be done. The conditions written into an employment contract can differ according to the position and the nature of work of a foreign employee.

Executive and managerial positions in Japanese companies are not usually available to foreigners unless those positions require highly specialized professional knowledge or technical skills that cannot be filled with equally competent Japanese nationals. This means that the foreign nationals will be hired on a contract as long as no Japanese replacements can be found. They are often expected to act as "tutors" for their Japanese colleagues and subordinates, and their actions are closely monitored. A robotics engineer who worked for a Japanese company explains his frustration: "In some cases, integration into a Japanese working group is impossible. Regardless of the reason (the person in question wasn't properly introduced, his alliances to other groups are suspect, his group is not well respected), involvement with that individual is on perceived benefit to the group. The group doesn't feel any responsibility to the individual and is often suspicious of his motives. Consequently, Japanese are often perceived as harsh and withholding."[5]

Foreigners should be aware that they will not be given real decision-making authority even in their own area of expertise. They will not find any explicit written rules and procedures that they can follow, although they will be assigned a mentor *(sewanin)*. This mentor can be one of the Westernized junior managers with a fairly good command of English, but the foreigner should not put complete trust in him or confide in him because he simply will not be allowed to keep a secret. Besides, he could be an outsider himself among others in his department. Foreigners should never publicly criticize any Japanese staff members no matter how incompetent and unreasonable they may seem. They will be ostracized if they are straightforward and honest in expressing their opinions of others.

Foreign employees at the management level are expected to socialize with other Japanese managers in the evenings and on weekends, and they are likely to be dragged into *habatsu arasoi* or "factional fights." Because many business matters are discussed and decided informally during social hours, it is almost impossible to catch up with what has been going on without spending many evenings in dining rooms and hostess bars and playing golf. Foreign

195

professionals must beware of unknowingly getting involved in interpersonal rivalries among dominant factions within the company. They should quickly identify the individual members of every faction and diplomatically decline to take sides with any faction. They should remain outsiders and always play "foreigners," and just perform their assigned tasks and duties.

The rapid economic development in recent years forced Japan to import foreign laborers (gaikokujin rōdōsha) to solve acute labor shortage in the construction, farming, fishery, and service industries. It is estimated that there are more than 300,000 laborers from the Philippines, Iran, Malaysia, Bangladesh, India, China, and even from South America. Many of these temporary foreign workers are illegal workers whose approved official term of stay has expired. The Japanese employers feel compelled to hire them (even with a fear of being fined for violation of the immigration law) because they cannot find enough Japanese nationals willing to work for low pay and under difficult work conditions. The majority of these men are working in heavy construction work, on farms as domestic animal keepers and fruit pickers, and in small factories as manual laborers. Almost all of the foreign women work in the service industry as golf caddies, cleaning women, waitresses, cooks, bar hostesses, and even as prostitutes. There are many reported cases of Filipino women who were promised good jobs, but forced to engage in prostitution by their Japanese employment agents. All these foreign laborers face discrimination at work. They are paid substandard wages and given few fringe benefits. They also face discrimination when they wish to rent an apartment. Japanese landlords are worried about creating a bad reputation in the neighborhood by renting to strange foreigners whose language, food habits, and social customs are vastly different from those of the Japanese tenants. In Japan's homogenous society, foreign laborers become very visible wherever they live, especially when they live in groups of several individuals. Some of the problems stem from the foreign workers' ignorance of the Japanese language and customs. Unscrupulous Japanese employment agents sometimes try to exploit them if they are ignorant about labor laws and work rules applicable to them. Japanese employers may even take advantage of their workers if they know that they are staying in Japan illegally beyond the authorized term of their work visa. Foreign workers should be careful not to put themselves in a difficult predicament. They should deal only with bona fide employment agents and should maintain their legal status as law-abiding temporary workers.

Japan's sports organizations actively recruit baseball players, sumo wrestlers, and soccer (football) players from foreign countries. Japanese professional baseball teams hire home-run hitters and pitchers from American major league teams to augment their teams' performance. However, based on a league agreement, no team can play more than two foreign players per game. Typically, most American baseball players come to Japan on a short contract. Sumo wrestlers from Hawai'i, Mongolia, and Brazil have reached top ranks and are enjoying the limelight in Japan. The tremendous popularity of the Japan Soccer League made the league owners recruit many talented foreign players from European and South American countries to help their Japanese teammates play better and more exciting games. These sports talents from foreign countries are "sports mercenaries" who are paid and treated well as long as they can perform at their best. Once they become unproductive, they will be dismissed almost immediately. The Hollywood movie *Mr. Baseball*, starring Tom Selleck, summarizes many of the typical frustrations that foreign sports talent faces in Japan.

Japanese universities, colleges, high schools, and junior high schools now hire native speakers of foreign language with the encouragement of the Japanese Ministry of Education. Universities and colleges hire many English instructors to teach English conversation, pronunciation and intonation. Those who want to teach at the college or university level must be native speakers of English and have a master's degree or a bachelor's degree from an accredited foreign university or college. Recently the Japanese Ministry of Justice authorized Japanese universities to hire foreign citizens on a permanent basis, but in practice, they offer only temporary positions for a one-year term with a renewal option for another year. In spite of this common employment practice, a good number of English teachers remain with their employers for ten years or more by renewing their contract year after year.[6]

Japanese high schools and junior high schools are now hiring English teachers under the Japan Language Teachers Program (JLT) sponsored by the Japanese Ministry of Education and the

197

Japanese Ministry of Foreign Affairs. The qualifications for this program are that prospective teachers have a four-year college degree, have good command of the language they will be teaching, and are under thirty-five years of age. Another requirement is that they are genuinely interested in Japanese culture and willing to help bridge the cultural gap between Japan and their own country.

The largest number of jobs available in this program is for English teachers, although it has recently created a small number of teaching positions for native speakers of Chinese, Korean, and other East Asian languages. It is estimated that some 2,500 English teachers are currently teaching in Japanese high schools and junior high schools. These English teachers are native speakers of English from the United States, Britain, Canada, Australia, or New Zealand. They are usually recent graduates from universities in their respective countries. Recruitment is coordinated through Japanese embassies and consulates so that applicants can apply for the positions in their home country. They are assigned to rural high schools or junior high schools as assistant English teachers to help Japanese English teachers there. Some of those who can speak good Japanese may be assigned to the international departments of local governments as coordinator for international relations, whose duties include coordinating visits of foreign visitors and planning and executing international programs.

There are a large number of private English conversation schools that hire thousands of native speakers of English. For example, one private English conversation school has 220 branches throughout Japan with a total student enrollment in excess of 60,000. The school hires hundreds of native speakers of English to teach students from kindergarten level to business-executive level. Working as an English teacher in Japan can provide an excellent opportunity to learn the Japanese language and to experience the culture and customs of Japan. Wages and benefits are fairly good for many of these teachers. In all cases, it is important to make sure that the Japanese employers provide free housing or subsidized housing because apartment or house rental fees are so expensive, especially in large cities like Tokyo and Osaka. It is also important to be aware that English teachers are "goldfish in a bowl" (cannot avoid the curious eyes of Japanese people), and that they cannot be too independent or liberal in attitude and behavior.

There is another way to live and work in Japan for young adults from Australia, New Zealand, and Canada. Currently, Japan has a mutual agreement with these countries that allows young men and women between eighteen and twenty-five years of age to work in Japan for one year on a special "working holidays" visa. The major objective of this visa is to promote mutual understanding and goodwill between participants and the host nationals through face-to-face contact in work situations. Many young Australians, New Zealanders, and Canadians live in Japan on this visa. Likewise, many young Japanese men and women live in these countries on this mutual agreement between their governments.

Notes

chapter 1

1. J. C. Condon, *With respect to the Japanese: A guide for Americans* (Yarmouth, Me.: Intercultural Press, 1984), pp. 39–40.

2. M. Imai, *Sixteen ways to avoid saying no: An invitation to experience Japanese management from the inside.* (Tokyo: Nihon Keizai Shimbun, 1982), pp. 6–8.

3. O. Mizutani, *Japanese: The spoken language in Japanese life*, trans. J. Ashby (Tokyo: The Japan Times, 1981), pp. 81–83.

4. T. S. Lebra, *Japanese patterns of behavior* Honolulu: (University of Hawai'i Press, 1976), pp. 123–124.

5. G. M. Chen, and W. J. Starosta, *Foundations of intercultural communication* (Needham Heights, Mass.: Allyn and Bacon, 1998), p. 25.

6. K. Nishiyama, *Japan-U.S. business communication* (Dubuque, Iowa: Kendall/Hunt, 1995), p. 3.

7. Ibid., p. 21.

8. U.S. Department of Commerce, press release (Dec. 8, 1981) (Washington, D.C.: U.S. Department of Commerce, 1982), pp. 4–5.

9. Lebra, *Japanese patterns of behavior,* pp. 28–30.

10. E. O. Reischauer, *The Japanese today: Change and continuity* (Cambridge, Mass.: Bellnap,1988), p. 166.

11. K. Schoolland, *Shogun's ghost: The dark side of Japanese education* (New York: Bergin and Garvey, 1990), pp. 107–117.

12. M. Imai, *Never take yes for an answer: An inside look at Japanese business for foreign businessmen* (Tokyo: The Simul Press, 1975), p. v.

13. Lebra, *Japanese patterns of behavior,* pp. 137–139.

chapter 2

1. E. J. Kaplan, *Japan: The government-business relationship—A guide for the American businessman* (Washington, D.C.: U.S. Department of Commerce, 1972), p. 14.

2. C. V. Prestowitz, Jr., *Trading places* (New York: Basic Books, 1988), p. 218.

3. K. Miyashita and D. W. Russell, *Keiretsu: Inside the hidden Japanese conglomerates* (New York: McGraw Hill, 1994), pp. 31–32.

4. G. S. Kikuchi, "What are *keiretsu* and why do some U.S. companies dislike them?" in *Japan—Why it works, why it doesn't: Economics in everyday life,* ed. J.Mak et al. (Honolulu: University of Hawai'i Press, 1998), pp. 185–186.

5. A. M. Whitehill, and S. Takezawa, *The other workers* (Honolulu: East West Center Press, 1968), p. 104.

6. E. T. Hall and M. R. Hall, *Hidden differences: Doing business with the Japanese* (New York: Anchor Books, 1987), p. 85.

7. Prestowitz, *Trading Places,* p. 293.

8. T. P. Rohlen, *For harmony and strength: Japanese white-collar organization in anthropological perspective* (Berkeley: University of California Press, 1974), pp. 34–40.

9. Nishiyama, *Japan-U.S. business communication,* pp. 52–54.

10. J. C. Abegglen, *The Japanese factory* (Glencoe, Ill.: Free Press, 1958), p. 27.

11. Ibid., p. 67.

12. S. B. Levine, *Industrial relations in postwar Japan* (Chicago, Ill.: University of Chicago Press, 1958), p. 18.

chapter 3

1. R. L. Tung, *Business negotiations with the Japanese* (Lexington, Mass.: Lexington Books, 1984), pp. 16–20.

2. M. J. Wolf, *The Japanese conspiracy: The plot to dominate industry worldwide—and how to deal with it* (New York: Empire Books, 1983), pp. 13–15.

3. R. M. March, *Honoring the customer: Marketing and selling to the Japanese* (New York: John Wiley, 1991), p. 11.

4. C. Brannen and T. Wilen, *Doing business with Japanese men.* (Berkeley: Stone Bridge Press, 1993), pp. 72–81.

chapter 4

1. J. Nist, "The language of the socially disadvantaged" in *Intercultural communication: A reader, 2nd ed.,* ed. L. A. Samovar and R. E. Porter, (Belmont, Calif.: Wadsworth, 1976), pp. 204–217.

2. C. V. Prestowitz, Jr., *Trading places: How we are giving our future to Japan and how to reclaim it* (New York: Basic Books, 1989), pp. 89–119.

3. R. M. March, *Honoring the customer,* pp. xv–xvii.

4. March, *Honoring the customer,* p.11.

5. K. Kobayashi, *Japan: The most misunderstood country* (Tokyo: Japan Times Publishing, 1985), p. 54.

chapter 5

1. J. L. Graham and Y. Sano, *Smart bargaining: Doing business with the Japanese* (New York: Harper Business, 1989), p. 17.

2. R. M. March, *The Japanese negotiator: Subtlety and strategy beyond Western logic* (Tokyo: Kodansha International, 1988), pp. 84–85.

3. Ibid., p. 130.

4. Graham and Sano, *Smart bargaining,* pp. 41–44.

5. Hall and Hall, *Hidden differences,* p. 109.

6. H. Van Zandt, "How to negotiate in Japan," *Harvard Business Review* , Nov.—Dec. 1972, pp. 45–46.

7. March, *The Japanese negotiator,* pp. 29–30.

8. M. Blaker, *Japanese international negotiation style* (New York: Columbia University Press, 1977), pp. 177–179.

9. Ibid., p. 202.

10. March, *The Japanese negotiator,* p. 129.

11. March, ibid., p. 26.

12. Lebra, *Japanese patterns of behavior,* pp. 80–81.

13. March, *The Japanese negotiators,* p. 22.

14. Graham and Sano, *Smart bargaining*, p. 24.

15. Ibid., p. 8.

16. March, *The Japanese negotiator*, p. 165.

17. March, ibid., p. 9.

18. March, ibid., pp. 141–142.

19. *Working with Japan: A practical guide to business success. Negotiating part 1: What to expect.* (Videotape lecture manual) (Carmel, Calif.: Intercultural Training Resources, 1992).

20. March, *The Japanese negotiator*, p. 112.

21. I. V. Hall, *Cartels of the mind: Japan's intellectual closed shop* (New York: W. W. Norton, 1998), pp. 21–33.

22. K. Nishiyama, *Communication in international business* (Tokyo: Sanshusha, 1981), pp. 188-189.

chapter 6

1. H. Glazer, *The international businessman in Japan* (Tokyo: Charles Tuttle, 1968), pp. 51-56.

2. M. Bairy, "Japanese ways," in *Doing business in Japan*, ed. R. J. Ballon, (Tokyo: Charles Tuttle, 1967), pp. 23-27.

3. T. F. M. Adams and N. Kobayashi, *The world of Japanese business* (Tokyo: Kodansha International, 1969), p. 70.

4. B. L. De Mente, *Japanese etiquette and ethics in business* (Lincolnwood, Ill. : Business Books, 1991), p. 166.

5. K. Noda, "Big business organization," in *Modern Japanese organization and decision-making,* ed. Ezra F. Vogel (Berkeley: University of California Press, 1975), pp. 115-116.

6. Ibid., 121–122.

7. De Mente, *Japanese etiquette,* p. 277.

8. Nishiyama, *Japan-U.S. business communication,* p. 73.

9. T. Kume, "Managerial attitudes toward decision-making," in *Communication, culture, and organizational process,* ed. W. B. Guydkunst, L. P. Stewart, and S. T. Toomey (Newbury Park, Calif.: Sage 1985), p. 235.

10. Ibid., p. 243.

11. De Mente, *Japanese etiquette,* 166.

chapter 7

1. Nishiyama, *Japan-U.S. business communication,* p. 203.

2. Ibid., p. 256.

3. A. H. Monroe, *Principles and types of speech* (New York: Scott Foresman & Company, 1949), p. 315.

4. H. L. Ewbank and J. Auer, *Discussion and debate* (New York: F. S. Crofts, 1941), p. 70.

chapter 8

1. P. Magnusson, J. B. Treece, and W. C. Symonds, "Honda: Is it an American car?" *Business Week,* Nov. 28, 1991, pp. 104-107.

2. S. P. Sethi, N. Namiki, and C. L. Swanson, *The false promise of the Japanese miracle* (Boston, Mass.: Pitman, 1984), pp. 192-194.

3. R. M. March, *Working for a Japanese company: Insights into the multinational workplace* (Tokyo: Kodansha International, 1992), p. 115. Nishiyama, *Japan-U.S. business communication,* p. 49.

4. J. K. Fukuda, *Japanese management in East Asia and beyond* (Hong Kong: The Chinese University Press, 1993), pp. 118-124.

5. Ibid., pp. 146-149.

6. C. Nakane, *Japanese society* (Berkeley: University of California Press, 1973), pp. 130-132.

7. Sethi, Namiki, and Swanson, *False promise,* pp. 67-68.

8. March, *The Japanese negotiators,* pp. 41-48.

9. Sethi, Namiki, and Swanson, *False promise,* p. 139; and March, *The Japanese negotiator,* pp. 116-121.

10. G. S. Roberts, *Staying on the line: Blue-collar women in contemporary Japan* (Honolulu: University of Hawai'i Press, 1994), p. 173.

11. Brannen and Wilen, *Doing business with Japanese men,* pp. 99-105.

12. T. Hamada, *American enterprise in Japan* (Albany, N.Y.: State University of New York Press, 1991). p. 213.

13. March, *The Japanese negotiator,* p. 112.

chapter 9

1. Lebra, *Japanese patterns of behavior,* p. 218.

2. Brannen and Wilen, *Doing business with Japanese men,* pp. 94-98.

3. The American Chambers of Commerce in Japan, *Living in Japan* *11th ed.* (Tokyo: IBI, 1993), pp. 167–168.

4. March, *The Japanese negotiator,* pp. 111–123.

5. P. Gercik, *On track with the Japanese: A case-by-case approach to building successful relationships* (New York: Kondansha International, 1992).

6. I. P. Hall, *Cartels of the mind: Japan's intellectual closed shop* (New York: W. W. Norton, 1998), pp. 80–108.

Glossary of Japanese Terms and Concepts

209

Index

214

215

About the Author

Kazuo Nishiyama is professor of intercultural communication at the University of Hawai'i. He has extensive experience living and teaching throughout Asia. He is the author of *Japan–U.S. Business Communication* and *Welcoming the Japanese Visitor: Insights, Tips, Tactics.*